FAD-FREE FOOD

Slimming with a Smile!

Trevor "Trim-Guy" Smith

Published by Sigma Leisure – an imprint of
Sigma Press, 1 South Oak Lane, Wilmslow, Cheshire SK9 6AR, England.

British Library Cataloguing in Publication Data
A CIP record for this book is available from the British Library.

ISBN: 1-85058-748-5

Typesetting and Design by: Sigma Press, Wilmslow, Cheshire.

Cover Design: The Agency, Macclesfield

Cartoons and cover illustration: Brian Sage

Printed by: MFP Design & Print

Foreword

by Rt Hon Menzies Campbell CBE QC MP

There is widespread concern today about the poor physical fitness of much of the British population, particularly young people, and the implications of this both for the future health and happiness of the British people and for the likely demands on the health service. The principal causes of this are recognised to be an unhealthy diet and lack of exercise.

As a former Olympic athlete I am well aware of the need to match food intake to the demands of physical exercise. When physical demands become less, as manual work in agriculture and heavy industry has given way to more sedentary employment, it is important to adjust calorie intake accordingly. The trick is to do this without reducing consumption of vitamins, fibre and other essential nutrients.

In "Fad-Free Food", Dr Smith shows us how to achieve a healthy regime without crash diets or dependence on whatever health food happens to be in fashion at the moment. As he says, the most important constituent of a balanced diet is food. Starving is not an option. There is no need to stop eating anything. Just get the balance right with plenty of fresh fruit and vegetables, and less high calorie foods.

All this good advice is written in a style that is fun to read. The humour and cartoons carry the reader along. This is a book that should be on every family's bookshelves.

Menzies Campbell
MP for North East Fife.

Dedication

This book is dedicated to my wife Janette and son, David
and to my parents – who always made me eat my greens.

Contents

Chapter 1

What "Fad-Free Food" Is All About

"Fad-Free Food" takes a fun look at the art of eating healthily and losing weight. "Don't be silly; how can losing weight possibly be fun? How can starving myself be fun? I like my food."

Well. I'll tell you. Healthy eating is fun because it doesn't mean eating less. It just means eating a wide range of healthy, low-fat foods and getting the balance right. It's fun, but there is a serious side too, so let's get that over right now in this paragraph and then we will be free to enjoy the rest of the book. The UK has one of the highest rates of premature heart disease in the world, largely because our diet is one of the world's worst. The crux of the matter is that Mr and Mrs Fat-Tooth and their kids eat far too much saturated fat, and too little fresh fruit and vegetables. It is up to the Fat-Tooths to ensure that they get a healthy diet. The aim of this book is to point the happy couple in the right direction and to get a few laughs along the road.

The World Health Organisation recommends that we should obtain no more than 10% of our energy from saturated fat, yet in the UK it currently contributes 16%. These are averages; it probably contributes even more to the Fat-Tooths' diet. Instead of obtaining it from fat, we should get over half of our energy from starchy foods like cereals and vegetables.

Recent UK government reports have presented further evidence of the inadequacies of our diet and made recommendations as to what changes need to be made. The official message to those of us living in the parts of the UK with the worst diets is encapsulated in the Ten Commandments reproduced below:

- ✔ Eat twice as much fresh fruit.
- ✔ Eat twice as many fresh and frozen vegetables.
- ✔ Increase the amount of bread you eat by half, all of the extra being wholemeal.
- ✔ Eat twice as much breakfast cereal.
- ✔ Reduce by a half the amount of processed meat and sausages you eat.
- ✔ Replace all of the whole milk you drink with semi-skimmed (except for children under the age of two years).
- ✔ Reduce the butter you eat by two thirds.
- ✔ Eat twice as much oily fish.
- ✔ Reduce the cakes, biscuits and pastry you eat by half.
- ✔ Reduce the amount of confectionery, soft drinks, and savoury snacks by a third for adults and a half for children.

"Who the heck do they think they are, telling me what to do?" do I hear you scream in defiance? No, they mean well; they have your interests at heart and an interest in your heart. So have a heart and give them a hearing.

Anyway, these are national targets and as an individual whether you need to double, quadruple, reduce by a half, or keep at the same level your consumption of a particular kind of food, will obviously depend on how much of it you eat at the moment. *Fad-Free Food* shows how, by always choosing the healthy, low-fat option, you may not need to reduce the amount of your favourite nibble at all. The overall government recommendations, however, provide an excellent guide as to what current medical opinion considers to be the healthiest foods that we should be eating most of and the not so healthy that we should eat only occasionally. Memorise the ten commandments and act on them. It is for your own good and indeed for the good of the planet. Apart from the one about eating more oily fish, the Commandments on the whole are pretty environmentally friendly.

The aim of *Fad-Free Food* is to help you choose, from the produce on sale at your local supermarket, town centre or corner shop, the best buys to facilitate the transition from a high fat to a moderate fat diet as painlessly as possible. Out of a dozen brands of breakfast cereal or baked beans some will be healthier than others. How do we choose the healthy option? Meat can be a healthy source of first-class protein or a slab of deadly saturated fat, depending on what kind of animal it comes from. How do we choose? Which are the healthy fats and which are the harmful and where are the different kinds found? What are the best kinds of fish to buy? Which dairy products can we continue to enjoy and which should we avoid? Why is excessive consumption of cakes and biscuits so bad for us? Should we give up eating eggs because of fears about cholesterol? What vitamins and minerals do we need, why do we need them and what kinds of food are they found in? Should all of the latest scares, BSE, E coli, genetically modified foods, leave us trembling in the supermarket aisles or are the risks exaggerated in the interests of a good story.

Fad-Free Food seeks to provide an answer to these questions and many, many more. Read the book, think about what it has to say, act on its advice and, most importantly, enjoy it!

Note: "Fad-Free Food" is intended as a general guide to healthy eating based on the standard advice of the Government's nutrition advisors. If you have any specific medical problems such as heart disease or diabetes, or are pregnant or very over- or under-weight, you should seek the advice of your family doctor or specialist.

Chapter 2

Eat Twice as Much Fresh Fruit

Let us make an imaginary visit to our favourite supermarket and see what fruit's on offer. Collect a trolley from the entrance and I'll lead the charge into the supermarket through the automatic doors. One of these days those doors aren't going to open and I'm going to end up with a trolley full of glass! Our journey through the typical supermarket starts with the fruit and vegetable section, just the place to come when we want a quick snack or desert! Most people in Britain eat far too little fruit. Health promoters recommended that we eat at least three portions of fruit the size of an apple or banana every day.

Experts can recommend until they are blue in the face but is there anyone out there willing to listen? In a recent survey carried out by the UK Department of Health, one in three of the people questioned admitted that they eat fresh fruit three times a **week** or less, let alone three times a **day**! It was a large-scale survey of over 16,000 people and can be taken as fairly representative of the population as a whole. Only one in five people said they eat fruit **more** than once a day. We clearly have a long way to go to achieve the Three a Day target and even further to achieve the healthy Mediterranean Diet where fresh fruit is eaten at virtually every meal and between meals.

The worst part of trying to attain the Trim-Guy image is not so much having to keep an eye on what food you buy yourself, but when your eye falls on what your fellow supermarketeers are filling their trolleys with. In the fruit and vegetable section, this is not a problem. Just buy what they do and more of it. Here are the things to go for.

Handy Apples

Aspiring Mr and Mrs Trim-Guy, this really is the fruit you *can* eat between meals without ruining your appetite, or greatly over-extending your waistline, so go for it.

Apples really are handy; you can pop them in your pocket or handbag – Mrs Trim-Guy, that is – without fear of ending up with a squashy mess by evening, and they are cheap – at least some varieties are. Price isn't related to nutritional value, so I always go for the cheapest. I actually prefer the crisp, clear taste of a Golden Delicious, although many connoisseurs would disagree with me. The apple is the ideal quick snack, so tear off a plastic bag and start collecting!

One of Britain's most popular apples is Cox's Orange Pippin. Good though it tastes, it is lower in vitamin C than some others. Sturmer Pippin has six times as much! This doesn't necessarily apply to other vitamins; the reverse may well be the case with Cox's having more of certain other valuable nutrients than Sturmer. As apple varieties vary so much in their vitamin and mineral content, to get the most that they have to offer get into the habit of buying lots of different varieties rather than sticking to the same one all of the time. The same principle applies to all fruit and vegetables. Unlike poor poverty-stricken me with my cheap Golden Delicious, eat a variety of varieties!

Should you wash apples before eating them? What if the apple in your hand dropped from its tree right into the middle of a cow pat before being harvested? Well, apples do get a bath in big tanks before they arrive in the supermarket and the harvesting of windfalls is frowned upon, but to be on the safe side give them a wash under the tap before lodging your teeth in them, or peel them. After all, you never know what dirty hands have been fingering them. Trouble with peeling apples, you lose some of the roughage and vitamins, but never fear, there is still a lot left. No need to worry about grub holes nowadays, as only the purest fruit reaches the supermarket shelves. The holey ones are fed to pigs, or used for making pies. In the olden days, there was only one thing worse than finding a grub in your apple: finding half a grub!

Pick up a Pear

Not so easy to pick up a pear if they are of the prickly variety, eaten for dessert in desert regions, and occasionally to be found on our supermarket shelves. These prickly pears which grow on the Opuntia cactus are in no way related to our familiar tree-growing fruit. Both dessert and cooking varieties of pears exist but virtually all of those offered for sale in the supermarket are dessert types. Although there are hundreds of varieties of pears, most supermarkets typically stock just two or three so our choice tends to be more limited than with apples. Pears have the annoying habit of taking a long time to get ripe and juicy and then going off quickly, but you can control the process to some extent with temperature. Putting them in a warm spot encourages ripening and once ripe the deterioration can be delayed for a few days by placing them in the refrigerator.

Pleasing Plums

Although they have only modest amounts of vitamin C, raw plums are very rich in beta-carotene from which we make vitamin A. More about that later. Choose plums which are quite firm and have a distinct bloom on the surface. If it's a rich, sweet flavour you go for, try the round, red Santa Rosa and the round, violet, Kirke's Blue. The Victoria and Japanese Plums in contrast are rather bland. Several varieties of plums are dried to produce prunes.

Perfect Peaches

Peaches may have white or yellow skins. The white-skinned varieties are generally sweeter. Choose fruit that is still quite firm but with no trace of greenness on the skin. If you are not ready to eat them immediately they can be kept for several days in the refrigerator. To make peaches easier to peel, pop them in boiling water for a few seconds first. Fresh peaches have about five times as much vitamin C as the canned varieties, which most of us tend to eat more of.

Happy Apricots

Apricots look like small peaches, round with yellow or orange skins. Pick the ones with the least wrinkled and darkest skins. If necessary, they can be ripened by leaving them in a warm room for a day or two. As with peaches, they can be skinned by plunging them into boiling water for a few seconds. Delicious fresh apricots have many other uses too. Inventive cooks stew them, poach them for serving with chicken, fill pies with them, and transform them into jam or even into wine. Canned peaches and apricots are user-friendly for people who have difficulty chewing, so long as they can open the cans.

Magnificent Melons

An excellent fruit much loved by rugby players who can't afford a proper ball. The trouble with the rugby ball-shaped Honeydew melons is that their tough skins make it difficult to tell if they are ripe or not. The smaller, rounder, Charantais, Ogen and especially the Cantaloupe melons generally have a sweeter, more fragrant taste, and it is easier to tell if they are ripe just by smelling them, or by doing the unthinkable and pressing the end of the melon to see if it gives or not. They also have more vitamin C and carotene.

Posh Pineapples

History has it that fifteenth-century Portuguese explorer Christopher Columbus and his pals were the first Europeans ever to taste a pineapple when they landed in Guadeloupe. The Indians of the Caribbean had been growing pineapples for ages. They didn't call them pineapples of course. They had a much more sensible name for them. They called them *nana*, which means 'flavour'; *nana, nana* 'flavour of flavours' from which its Latin name, *Ananas comosus* is derived. You know this guy Linnaeus, who developed the system of giving Latin names to animals and plants, well that wasn't his real name. It was Karl von Line. He Latinised his own name as well!

Once a food only wealthy folk could afford, pineapples are now within the pocket of most of us, at least as a special treat. The best way of choosing a pineapple is to smell it to make sure that it has the characteristic pineapple aroma. After devouring the fruit, it is fun to plant the leaves in a mixture of sand and peat covered with a clear plastic bag as a makeshift propagator to try and grow them on as an ornamental plant.

Bananarama

Bananas look curvy. They taste curvy too. Along with apples, the fruit we buy most of is the banana. Did you know that 600,000 tons of bananas are eaten in Great Britain every year, and did you know that if you laid all of the bananas grown in the world end to end they would encircle the globe more than 2,000 times? Wow, what a mine of useless information! Fuelled with twice as much carbohydrate as most other fruits, and consequently energy to the tune of around 100 kcal, a banana makes an ideal energy-rich snack. Just a little bit fattening perhaps, but who cares when it is so full of natural goodness. For many people in the tropics bananas are more than just a snack, they are their staple diet and livelihood. Only about a tenth of the 75 million tonnes produced annually are exported. Many of the world's biggest producers, including India, Mexico and Indonesia, don't export a lot, they keep them for themselves, and who can blame them.

Lemons, Limes and the Dreaded Scurvy

Citrus fruits share a common bond: they are all members of the exclusive vitamin C club. The dreaded scurvy had been decimating ships' crews on their long voyages of discovery and severely depleting the fighting strength of the British navy. A sailor with scurvy was depressed, weak and anaemic, and not at all in the mood for fighting the French, or anyone else for that matter. Then, just as the French thought their luck was in, in 1747 a Royal Navy surgeon by the name of James Lind discovered the remarkable anti-scurvy properties of the lemon. Lind got hold of some scurvy victims and divided them into groups, and fed each group differently, very much as nutritionists would carry out a controlled experiment today. The group of patients whose diet included two oranges and a lemon made a remarkable recovery in just a few days. Lind's work went on to establish that green vegetables as well as citrus fruits would prevent and cure scurvy, the advantage of citrus fruits being that they and their juice would keep longer on a long sea voyage in an age when refrigerators were still to be invented.

After a minor delay of half a century, in 1795 the British Admiralty decreed that every British seaman should be provided with a daily dose of citrus fruit. It has been said that, "Lind, as much as Nelson, broke the power of Napoleon." Lind didn't call them lemons; he called them limes, which is why British sailors came to be called limeys. What we call limes today are not lemons but a different kind of citrus fruit. In case you were wondering, the lime trees that line the driveways of stately homes do not produce limes. They just happen to have the same name. Confusing isn't it.

Lemons are an ancient fruit cultivated by the Chinese 3,000 years ago, so they probably knew all about their health-giving properties long before we did. Most of we landlubbers today will plumb for less bitter methods of getting our vitamin C, but lemons are still much sought after for creating such culinary delights as lemon meringue pie, and the juice is very useful for keeping sliced apples and bananas looking fresh in the lunch box. If you want the tang of real lemon juice you are as likely to find it in washing up liquid as in lemonade.

Glorious Grapefruit

An altogether more palatable citrus fruit, and just as rich in vitamin C as the lemon, is the grapefruit, the elephant of the citrus world. The largest of the citrus fruits, it is an essential start to the day for many people. Choose shiny and heavy fruit that give slightly when pressed. You can store them for a few weeks in a cool place. In the nineteenth century enterprising farmers set up commercial grapefruit plantations in America using seed and plants from the Bahamas. So successful were they that grapefruit exports soon became a major source of revenue for the states of Arizona, California and Texas. Then, at the beginning of the twentieth century the grapefruit crossed the Atlantic and arrived in Palestine where large orchards were planted. A truly international fruit, the grapefruit in your hand may have hailed from either side of the Atlantic.

Grapefruit diets come into fashion every few years. Adherents eat a grapefruit with every meal or between meals and lose weight – if they are lucky. So long as you eat less of other things as a result of being filled up by the grapefruit you may well lose weight, but there is no magic chemical in grapefruit that in itself is likely to initiate a weight loss. Irrespective of whether or not they help us to shed pounds, grapefruits are part of a healthy diet, so long as we steadfastly resist the temptation to blanket them with sugar.

Ordinary Oranges

Oranges were first imported into Britain from Spain at the end of the thirteenth century and were re-introduced by Sir Walter Raleigh in the sixteenth. Spuds and oranges. Did any one man ever do more to change the British way of life? Pity all of his introductions were not so healthy. I am, of course, referring to tobacco. Rich in vitamin C and other vitamins, orange juice is now abundant and as much a part of many people's diets as milk used to be. Have you noticed, though, how the pips in oranges seem to be getting rarer? If you want the pleasure of planting pips in pots and watching them grow, better get planting now before total sterility sets in.

La Nouvelle Exotica

Pineapples, bananas and the citrus fruits were all exotic fruits in their day. One can imagine people's reaction to them when they were first introduced into Britain. Fast becoming so familiar in the supermarket as to be in imminent danger of losing their exotic image too are kiwi fruit and mangoes, both of which are excellent sources of vitamin C.

The word 'kiwi' conjures up a picture of a small flightless bird trotting through New Zealand woodlands, but despite its name the kiwi fruit originated not in New Zealand but in China. It was not until early in the twentieth century that it embarked in New Zealand, after which it was extensively planted and rose to become one of the country's major agricultural exports. It was renamed the kiwi fruit by the New Zealanders in 1959, although it is still often known by its earlier and more descriptive name of Chinese gooseberry.

Not so long ago mangoes were a rarity, but today they are found in most supermarkets, and the choice of varieties is increasing. Most people enjoy the texture, which is reminiscent of peaches, along with the unique mango taste. As a bonus, at the centre of the fruit is this very interesting seed encased in what looks like a purse, which gives them extra appeal for children. Have you been mango'd? If not, give one a try.

Custard apple, granadilla, guava, kiwano, kumquat, lychees, mangosteen, pomello, passion fruit, paw paw, piahaya, physalis, prickly pear, rambuttan, sharon fruit, star fruit, ugli fruit. Is there no end to the list of exotic fruits with unpronounceable names appearing on our supermarket shelves? Give vent to your inborn spirit of adventure and try something new this week. A single fruit doesn't cost much so if you find you can't stand the taste it's no great loss. On the other hand, you might hit the jackpot and discover a new fruit to go on enjoying for years.

Beautiful Berries and Cute C-rich Currants

As citrus fruits are a much richer source of vitamin C than home-grown apples and pears, how did earlier inhabitants of these isles manage to obtain sufficient vitamin C before the development of trade links with other parts of the world? The answer is 'with great difficulty.' Despite the absence of photographs and video cameras in mediaeval times, artists of the day have provided us with many faithful representations of the features of their subjects. In certain cases, these portraits show clear evidence of scurvy. In a cold, damp year when fresh fruit and vegetables were in short supply many people suffered it seems from the effects of a lack of vitamin C.

Let it not be imagined, however, that warm, sunny climates have a monopoly of fruits with high vitamin C levels. Strawberries have more vitamin C weight for weight than oranges and they grow wild around the world, including the chilly Alps. The snag is that in the cool British climate the season for home-grown berries is very short and if it is a bad season, producing no surplus for preserving as jam, deficiencies could easily arise during the winter months. Twentieth-century technology ensures that this situation need not arise in Britain today as ships and planes follow the sun, importing vitamin C-rich fruit and vegetables from around the world, summer or winter, come rain or shine.

Soft home-grown fruits like gooseberries, blackberries, raspberries and loganberries are all rich in vitamin C. In the days when small fields and dense hedgerows were the norm, blackberries were a much more prominent feature of the British countryside than they are now. Gooseberries, though not a native species, were used for hedging in mediaeval gardens. Present day raspberry varieties read like a map of Scotland – Glen Moy, Glen Prosen, Glen Lyon – just a few of the 500 or so varieties held at the Scottish Crop Research Institute near Dundee. First prize for the highest vitamin C content, however, goes to the humble blackcurrant, which contains an unbelievable four times as much vitamin C as the same weight of oranges. Being a bit tart to the taste buds, messy to eat, and available for only a short period of the year, cartons of blackcurrant juice are a more convenient source of vitamin C nowadays than the currants themselves.

It is not only for their vitamin C that blackberries, raspberries, blackcurrants are to be prized. Berries and currants are also an excellent source of fibre, sporting about three times as much as most other fruits. Other types of single berries have also started to appear on the supermarket shelves including blueberry, a great favourite in the

United States. It is one of a family of berries that include the huckleberry, bilberry, whortleberry and cranberry. The name of the cranberry, better known for its juice than as a berry for eating, is derived from the shape of the blossom which is said to be reminiscent of a crane's neck, if you can remember what a crane's neck looks like.

The grape is another soft fruit with a great deal to offer, even for teetotallers. As well as vitamins (although they are a bit short on vitamin C), grapes are also a good source of minerals, as the vines, being deep-rooted, can draw up minerals from deep below the soil long after the top soil has become depleted.

Most kinds of berries are rich in vitamin C and fibre, but unless we really know for certain that they are safe to eat the supermarket shelf rather than the hedgerow is the safest place to gather them.

Frankenstein Fruit

The interbreeding of different varieties of a plant, like maize for instance, to produce varieties with new desirable characteristics, such as disease resistance or ease of harvesting, has been practised for hundreds of years. With some of the fruit on our supermarket shelves the trend has gone one step further with the interbreeding not only of different varieties but also of different species to produce Frankenstein Fruit.

Nearly a century after the appearance of Mary Shelley's famous yarn in 1818, the clementine was generated as a result of across between a mandarin and a sweet orange in the garden of Father Pierre Clement in Algeria. Then came the minneola, alias the tangelo or orlando, a cross between the tangerine and the grapefruit. It gets worse; the Ugli fruit is a three way cross between a grapefruit, orange and tangerine. It was first bred in Jamaica and the name, Ugli, was patented by Jamaica Produce.

Soft fruits have been subject to similar treatment. The loganberry, named after J.M. Logan who did much of the development work at the start of the century, is a cross between a blackberry and a raspberry. The tayberry is a product of Anglo-American co-operation. Developed at the Scottish Crop Research Institute near Dundee, in an area known as Tayside, it arose from a cross between a particular type of American blackberry and a Scottish raspberry. There is even a four-way cross. The boysenberry, derived in France in the 1920s, is said to be a cross between a strawberry, raspberry, loganberry and dewberry.

A Pair of Ill-fitting False Teeth

It's all very well for me to sing the virtues of tucking into lots of fresh fruit, but what if you have a pair of ill-fitting choppers, decayed teeth or inflamed gums and can't bite into an apple or carrot without experiencing the agony of aching teeth and gums. In that case, pre-mastication is the answer. Give your gums a break and reduce the raw fruit and vegetables to a pulp before they enter the dark portal that is your mouth.

Cut the apple into very thin slices, as though you were going to examine its cellular structure under a microscope, or grate it. A cheese grater will do. The same goes for carrots, turnips and any other hard fruit or vegetable. Grate it first. For anyone who has trouble chewing a banana, a fork is a handy implement. Mashed banana tastes delicious and the transformation in texture produced by a few downward strokes of the fork is truly remarkable. For people who have difficulty chewing, soft fruit such as

fully ripe peaches and pears are a good alternative. Berries and currants are obviously very soft but the seeds and other hard bits might get behind the falsies and cause problems. Most canned fruit is soft and the little cubes in cans of mixed fruit are easy to digest. Once boiled, most vegetables are soft and easy to digest. People who eat less fruit because of problems with chewing should top up with fruit and vegetable juices. You could also exploit the wonders of modern technology and use an electric blender. Even for the gummiest amongst us there is no excuse for not eating plenty of fresh fruit and vegetables.

Canned Fruit

A dark, damp, metal prison from which there is no escape. What did they do to deserve such a fate? (A good opening for a novel that.) Despite the heroic prose, canned fruit is almost as good as the real thing; it adds variety and can make a tasty snack. The main problems are that canned fruit often contains added sugar and you are paying as much for the can as you are for its contents. All it not lost, however, as most manufacturers now offer a choice: the same product bathed, for the sweet-toothed (if they have not all decayed away!), in sugary syrup or, for the weight watcher, in fruit juice, though not necessarily their own. For example, you can buy peach halves in sugar and glucose syrup at around 70 kcal per 100g or alternatively in juice at around 50 kcal. Go for the juicy rather that the syrupy ones. The fact that, as likely as not, the peaches will be bathed not in peach juice but in pineapple juice is neither here nor there. If anything, you get a wider range of nutrients that way.

Dried Fruit

They tend to be dry in taste but are a useful standby for when you don't have any fresh fruit in the house. The small packets of reconstituted apricots and other fruit are great for the school lunchbox and a less fattening alternative to snack bars and crisps. Drop in some currants and raisins too.

Fruit Juice as Pure as the Girl of Your Dreams

Nowadays, at least some of the benefits of fresh fruit can be obtained without actually eating them. Don't forget the fibre though; we miss out on that. The production of pure fruit juice has become a major industry in many countries in recent years and we are now spoiled for choice. No longer limited to the tiny glass bottles of orange and pineapple juice available behind the bar, we can now buy orange, grapefruit, pineapple, grape, tomato, and mixtures of exotic fruit juices by the litre carton – six at a time if we want to save cash.

Pure fruit juice is an excellent drink. It is a great source of energy for a start. Sporting between 10 and 12 per cent healthy natural sugar, citrus fruit juices are ideal as an energy-rich snack. They are so much better than sticky chocolate bars that contain masses of saturated fat as well as the sugar. Did you know that there is as much energy in a litre carton of pure orange juice as in two snack-sized Mars Bars?

Pure fruit juice is virtually fat free. Like the whole fruit, it is a rich source of vitamin C, a small glass (150ml) containing half the recommended daily level. It doesn't matter whether you drink grapefruit juice or orange juice, all citrus juices are rich in vitamin C.

Fruit Juice Drinks

Beware of imitations. A carton of orange, apple or other drink if it consists of pure unadulterated juice will state so on the label. The words *pure juice* or at least *pure* must appear somewhere on the carton, otherwise what you are buying will almost certainly not be pure juice. If pure juice is what you want, always make sure that is exactly what it is stated to be. No other words will do. Don't be deceived by similar-sized cartons with pictures of oranges and blackcurrants, announcing themselves as a 'fruit juice drink', 'crush' or just 'orange drink'. The expression 'juice drink' almost always means: a little juice, and a lot of water. So before you buy a 'juice drink', ask yourself whether you would be better off buying *pure* juice instead. It is unlikely to be much more expensive, especially if you buy a large carton instead of a pack of smaller ones.

Most juice sold in family-size, one litre cartons is pure juice although there are some prominent exceptions. Ribena blackcurrant juice drink and tropical juice drinks such as Five Alive are two of them. Both have water added, but as they also contain a good helping of fruit juice, and would be too bitter if served neat, they cannot be faulted and are worth drinking.

In contrast to the family-sized cartons, most of the drinks sold in snack-sized cartons with an integral straw are fruit juice drinks rather than pure juice. There are over a hundred types of these 250ml cartons of fruit juice drinks currently on the market, often suitably festooned with cartoon characters on the box to appeal to children.

So if fruit juice drinks do not consist of pure fruit juice what do they consist of? Basically water, sugar or artificial sweeteners, colourings and flavourings. By law, a juice drink must contain fruit juice but it doesn't need to contain more than 5 per cent. The rest can be, and usually is, water and sugar! In practice, most brands contain more than the minimum 5 per cent juice but few have more than 20 per cent, and many still do not come clean and state on the label exactly how much juice they do contain. A welcome exception to the let's-get-away-with-as-little-as-possible rule tends to be the supermarkets' own brands of orange juice drinks that often contain up to a half of fruit juice. One well-known store positions theirs next to the pure juice and craftily calls it *Lite* Orange Drink. Of course it's light, half of it is water!

When you buy a fruit juice drink, what you are paying for is a small amount of fruit juice dissolved in water, with vitamin C and sugar added to make up for what was in the missing fruit. Diet varieties of fruit juice drinks have artificial sweeteners added instead of the sugar. Some fruit juice drink manufacturers go over the top in replenishing their diluted fruit juices with lost vitamins, adding vitamins such as B12 and D that weren't there in the first place, and that never occur naturally in fruit (unless you include the caterpillars).

It is not that there is anything particularly harmful about juice drinks. A small amount of juice in infinitely better than no juice at all. Blackcurrant and cranberry juice are very rich and do not have to be taken neat. Ten per cent of their juice in a glass of water is quite a lot of juice and compares favourably with the amount we would be likely to consume if we helped ourselves directly from the bush, even if we had a mythical bush in our garden which bore fruit all year round.

But when it comes to orange juice, why pay good money for water and sugar when the pure juice, if you buy it in bulk, can actually cost less. Most supermarkets sell their own brand of orange juice at a lower price per litre than packs of three 250ml cartons of fruit juice drink. For the school lunch box you can save a pound or two a month by pouring your children pure juice from a litre carton into a plastic flask rather than giving them disposable 250ml cartons of juice drink, and improve their nutrition to boot. If you have several children, why not dilute the pure juice with water to make it even more economical. Pure juice can be diluted with an equal volume of water without losing too much of its taste and without the need to add extra sugar or artificial sweetener. A glass of warm diluted pure orange juice makes a delicious bedtime drink for all the family.

Dentists jump up and down at the prospect of children eating too many sweets and sipping too many sweet drinks between meals. At the risk of being blacklisted by the British Dental Association – I'm not a dentist so who cares – despite dental advice, who would want to discourage children from enjoying such an eminently healthy snack as pure fruit juice? It is so much better than most of the alternatives such as crisps and snack bars that contain too much nasty saturated fat. Let's compromise, drink the juice and brush our teeth afterwards.

The take home message is – always point your trolley in the direction of the *pure* fruit juice, rather than the more insipid fruit juice drinks or bottles of squash for diluting. Most importantly, try to avoid loitering around those cans of fizzy drinks, many of which contain no fruit juice at all, just chemical flavourings.

Caught in a Jam

Jam is a traditional method of preserving fresh fruit so that its benefits remain available long after it is out of season. As it retains much of the vitamin C of the fresh fruit it probably helped to save thousands of people in the recent past from the misery of scurvy. Today, with fresh fruit and vegetables available in our supermarkets and greengrocers all year round, and vitamin C trapped in cartons of orange juice, as well as turning up in all sorts of unlikely places as an additive, jam does not have quite the same healthy status. Despite this, so long as it is not overdone there is no reason why it should not provide a tasty addition to our diet. Jam's problem is that it has too much sugar, that already present in the fruit being swamped by the refined sugar added as a preservative. About half of a typical jar of jam is sugar, but as sugar has less than half as many calories as the same weight of fat, and as there is no fat in jam to speak of, the number of calories is less than you might think. One hundred grams of jam provides about 250 kcal, just half what you get from the same weight of Kit Kat or Mars bars, so you may be able to get away with a thin layer of jam on a slice of brown bread occasionally, when I'm not looking.

Jams with a reduced sugar content are available, but never take a claim of *reduced sugar* at its face value. Always read the nutrition information first. You may well find a brand of 'reduced sugar strawberry jam' that has slightly more sugar than another brand that makes no such claim about being reduced. In any case, *reduced sugar* usually just means that the jar is about one third sugar instead of the traditional one half. Jam, by definition, is sugar rich. In diabetic jams, the sugar is replaced by an equal weight of sorbitol, a bulk sweetener used in many diabetic foods. For those who do not have diabetes, sorbitol is unlikely to offer any advantage.

Chapter 3

Eat Twice as Many Fresh and Frozen Vegetables

That's what the experts say. The advice is directed to the British population as a whole, of course, not necessarily to you or me. It depends on how many vegetables we eat at the moment. If you eat hardly any vegetables, maybe you should eat five times as many, or maybe you already eat lots and do not need any extra. In reality, few of us eat so many vegetables that we would not benefit from eating more of them. In the Department of Health's survey mentioned earlier, two out of three people reported eating vegetables every day, so we obviously do a lot better with vegetables than we do with fruit. Even so, one in ten people said they eat vegetables less than three times a week. We still have a long way to go, therefore, to achieve the official recommendation that we should eat at least five helpings of fruit and vegetables every day.

A prize for whoever can invent the corniest slogan. How about this for starters?

Five a day is the healthy way
So let's go for five
And stay alive!

Casting the Spotlight on Spuds

No supermarket vegetable section would be complete without a ton or so of what was for long the staple diet of millions of people in Britain and Ireland. Yes, you've got it, the potato. Introduced from South America in the sixteenth century, potatoes eventually became the main source of carbohydrate and protein for large sections of the population. Then disaster struck in the shape of potato blight, which year after year obliterated much of the crop. Thousands starved while others migrated to America. This tragedy illustrates the importance of not relying too heavily on just one or two sources of food, excellent as they might be.

Many different varieties of potatoes are grown on our farms. Varieties high in starch and low in sugar are preferred for crisp and chip making, while canners require small varieties of potatoes that are low in starch with a waxy flesh to withstand the canning process. Other varieties are chosen for their resistance to drought or disease.

Most of the cereal crop arrives in our kitchen as bread, breakfast cereal, cakes and biscuits, in other words, processed to a greater or lesser degree. In contrast, the bulk of the potato crop – over two thirds – from British farms is sold to the consumer as natural raw potato. Wonderful! Potatoes, like root vegetables and cereals, are an excellent source of the starch from which, as we shall see later, we should be obtaining most of our energy.

As well as satisfying our need for energy-yielding starch, potatoes are also an excellent source of vitamin C. New potatoes straight from the soil have at least half as much vitamin C weight for weight as citrus fruits. Not everyone knows that. The amount of the vitamin falls with storage and still more can be squandered by overzealous boiling, but even so, as we British and Irish tend to eat cartloads of spuds, they serve as a significant, inexpensive, natural source of vitamin C for millions of us.

Now for the bad news. We now buy a third less raw potatoes than we did twenty years ago, despite the fact that most of us now have a big metal trolley powered by an infernal combustion engine to carry them and ourselves home in. Oops, I've ended the sentence with a preposition. That reminds of the time I was wondering around a university campus looking for the library. I approached a student and asked, "Excuse me, would you be good enough to tell me where the library is at?"

The student, in a very arrogant and belittling tone, replied, "I am sorry, but at this university we are taught never to end a sentence with a preposition!"

I bit my tongue, smiled, and in a very apologetic tone replied, "I beg your pardon. Please allow me to rephrase my question. Would you be good enough to tell me where the library is at, pompous twit?"

Back to the spuds. They are an inexpensive, highly nutritious part of our diet, so if you, prospective Mr and Mrs Trim-Guy, are among those responsible for the falling consumption, think again!

Smashing Mash

If it's a bit laborious eating lots of solid potato, why not mash them. Cut the potato up into small chunks; place in a pan of boiling water, cover with the lid and simmer until tender. Drain, return to the pan and add hot, semi-skimmed milk. To make the potato even tastier add some crushed garlic, pesto or fresh herbs. Mashed potato is also a highly nutritious food for people who have difficulty chewing.

When the Chips are Down

What about chips, chaps? The chip, that Great British contribution to world cuisine, is a nutritionist's nightmare, a classic example, like crisps, of how to convert the superbly healthy potato into something far less desirable. But The Fat-Tooth Family just loves them. As well as being a health hazard, fat-filled chip pans are a serious fire hazard. They are one of the commonest causes of house fires, so hand yours in at the local fire station to be painlessly destroyed. Having disposed of the chip pan, we can now reveal that many of the brands of frozen oven-ready chips threatening, cuckoo fashion, to displace everything else from the supermarket freezers contain less than 5 per cent fat overall and less than 1 per cent of the harmful, saturated kind, so eaten in moderation they are not really that bad. You will be hearing a lot more about the horrors of saturated fat later. Oven-readies are certainly a great improvement on the freshly-fried chips so often served up in chippies and some restaurants and those typically prepared at home, which are usually plastered with saturated fat and should carry a government health warning. Many independent restaurants nowadays offer a more varied menu, but in most fast food restaurants, it is still fries with everything. Desperate for somewhere to eat, I went into a McDonald's the other evening and asked for some fries. The girl at the counter asked, "Would you like some fries with that?"

Getting to the Root of the Problem

All root crops – turnips, swedes, mangel-wurzels, beetroot, carrots, parsnips etc. – are, like potatoes, an inexpensive source of the starch from which the World Health Organisation tells us we should be obtaining most of our energy. As a bonus, they also contain a variety of vitamins and minerals, a respectable amount of protein, and a good deal of fibre to keep our bowels moving. In case you have always wondered but were afraid to ask, yes, swedes did come to Britain from Sweden, towards the end of the eighteenth century, having originated in Bohemia.

With the size and texture of ten-pin bowling balls, raw swedes and turnips tend to attract a limited clientele. This is a pity when there are so many tasty, bite-size varieties available. So long, however, as there is a carpenter in the family who can hack their way through the turnip reducing it to boilable chunks, turnips make an excellent dinner vegetable. With the recent introduction to the vegetable section of miniature varieties of sweetcorn, cabbages, carrots, and even mini turnips in some supermarkets, we will soon be able to return the vice, hacksaw, hammer and chisel to their rightful place in the tool shed. Joking apart, once chopped up into small chunks and boiled, the bowling ball turnips become soft and tasty and well worth the effort.

Happily, slim guy parsnips and carrots are no trouble at all to prepare. They are two of the few things we eat nowadays which are indigenous to Britain. The wild varieties though are very much smaller than their well-bred relatives. If not organically grown, we just need to peel, and top and tail them to get rid of any pesticide residues and there we are. We should eat more of these highly nutritious, vitamin-rich roots. Be eco-friendly and boil them in the same pot as the potatoes and save on the washing up into the bargain.

Carrots are a particularly interesting vegetable as they are a major source of a substance called beta-carotene which our bodies can convert into vitamin A. It is this beta-carotene which makes carrots more orange than oranges. Extracted carotenes are often used to colour other kinds of food. As well as being an antioxidant (more about antioxidants later), vitamin A is essential for the proper functioning of the eyes. In many parts of the world, vitamin A deficiency is a major cause of blindness, a needless tragedy as it can so easily be prevented, even where the diet is poor, by supplements of the vitamin. Substances made from vitamin A also help us to see in the dark. I will spare you the old joke about rabbits never being seen wearing glasses!

Beta-carotene is absorbed from our intestines better in the presence of fat, so make a habit of adding some grated carrot to any dish you prepare using vegetable oil or to a dish which is to be followed by small amounts of a fatty dessert like ice cream. Carrots do not, of course, have to be cooked. There are lots of very tasty varieties that we can eat raw, grated or, if we like a good crunch, just as they are.

The good news is that although the consumption of potatoes has fallen, that of other fresh vegetables including carrots and parsnips (with the possible exception of the evocative mangel-wurzel) has remained steady. But on reflection, that is not really such good news. Consumption should be rising, not remaining steady at an already pathetically low level.

The really bad news is that there is one root vegetable that most of us continue to eat far too much of; and that is, yes you've guessed it, that close relative of the beetroot, sugar beet. In contrast to other root crops, a high percentage of its carbohydrate is not starch but sugar, which after being extracted and put into bags, we spoon into our tea. People who are as refined as the sugar pour it into a fancy sugar bowl first and then spoon it gracefully into their tea. The Fat-Tooths tip it into their tea directly from the bag without bothering with a spoon at all. The sugar poured from much bigger bags into cakes and biscuits, breakfast cereals and cans of fruit and vegetables by the manufacturers is actually even more of a problem than that we buy ourselves. Apart from this one black sheep – or should it be white sheep – of the family, root crops provide us with energy-giving starch, vitamins, fibre and a fair amount of protein. Roots are good for us and we should resolve to eat more of them, so get digging.

An Abbreviated History of Medicine
(Why is abbreviated such a long word?)

Odd isn't it, how history comes full circle. Today, everyone, deep down, realises the benefits of healthy eating, even if they don't practise it. Eat healthily and you will stay fit and healthy. Here then is a short history of medicine to see how we have arrived at this conclusion.

- ☛ 2000BC – "Here, eat this root."
- ☛ AD1000 – "That root is heathen, say this prayer."
- ☛ AD1850 – "That prayer is superstition, drink this potion."
- ☛ AD1940 – "That potion contains arsenic, swallow this pill."
- ☛ AD1985 – "That pill is ineffective, take this new pill."
- ☛ AD2000 – "That pill does more harm than good. Here, eat this root; it contains lots of starch, protein, vitamins and fibre and guarantees a long, healthy life."

2000 BC   2000 AD

Eat your Greens

Now for the greens. I hope you always eat your greens. Some people think that green vegetables are God's way of letting mothers get their own back on their children. But greens don't have to be tasteless, soggy and vitamin depleted; they should be crisp, tasty and highly nutritious. What do we get from greens? Not a lot of starch and very little protein, but they are an excellent source of roughage and certain very important vitamins. These vitamins include beta-carotene, vitamin C and folic acid. This last named vitamin is essential during pregnancy. In fact, supplements are often automatically prescribed by doctors on the cheeky assumption that mothers-to-be are not eating their greens. Remember that the amount you obtain of any vitamin or mineral depends not only on how much the vegetable contains in every ounce, but on how much is lost in cooking before you eat it and how much of it you actually eat. Parsley is very rich in vitamin C, but because we tend to eat so little of it, it is not likely to contribute significantly towards our total intake of the vitamin. Potatoes on the other hand, although they only have about a tenth as much vitamin C as the same weight of parsley, provide us with a substantial amount of the vitamin because we eat so many of them.

Lettuces and Cabbages – such big hearts and so generous with their vitamin C

My favourite green leafy vegetable is lettuce. I love brown lettuce sandwiches. It's the bread that's brown, not the lettuce, of course! The great advantage of lettuce over most leafy vegetables is that it is usually eaten raw without any of the beta-carotene (which we can convert into vitamin A) and vitamin C being lost as a result of cooking. A point to remember is that with lettuces and cabbages the green outer leaves have several times more vitamin C than the white inner leaves, so eat both.

Chinese cabbages, like lettuces, can be eaten as a salad vegetable and are now available in most supermarkets. In case you have any qualms about Chinese methods of fertilising the soil – Sh.. you know what! – Chinese refers to the variety rather than the immediate country of origin. British cabbages, both red and green, can be eaten raw too. They can be grated and added to salads along with grated carrots, apples and so on, but for some reason they usually end up boiled. A pound of *raw* cabbage contains as much vitamin C as a pound of oranges. Better still, Brussels sprouts have twice as much! To avoid losing most of the vitamin C it is important to remember to boil for as short a time and in as little water as possible. Why not go one step further and re-use the water for making soup, or just drink it neat, rather than pour its precious vitamins and minerals down the drain.

The ancestors of the supermarket lettuces and cabbages still grow wild, but the wild varieties are nowhere near as huge and football-like as the iceberg lettuces and cabbages of the supermarket. Modern day icebergs are the result of years of selective breeding to produce as much green leaf on as small an area of land as possible. This strategy has obviously proven very successful and provided us with the not-to-be-missed opportunity of making a substantial helping of green leaves a regular part of our diet.

Cauliflower is also a good buy. Pound for pound it too, when fresh, has even more vitamin C than oranges. A boiled cauliflower and grated, half-fat cheese makes an excellent light meal. Not too much cheese though and go gently with the boiling.

Spinach is another leafy vegetable that is readily obtainable, and has the reputation for being a good source of iron. All greens have a fair amount of iron but spinach has about three times as much iron as most other vegetables. Unfortunately, the iron in spinach is in a form that it is difficult for us to absorb from our intestines. Spinach can still hold its head high though, because it is also very rich in beta-carotene for making vitamin A. Pound for pound it is one of the richest sources after carrots. Curly kale and red peppers also have exceptionally large amounts of beta-carotene.

Dandelion

Dandelion is a native green found growing throughout Britain on every garden path. This once-popular food plant is greatly under-utilised nowadays. The French name for dandelion is pis-en-lit, which literally means pee-the-bed, and refers to its diuretic properties. It's not that bad though so don't be put off eating it on that account. As well as providing leaves for salads, dandelion roots are used as a coffee substitute on sale in health food shops.

Nose Twisters

Another green that grows wild in parts of Britain is watercress, although as most inland water is contaminated with cow dung, if not industrial chemicals, care has to be taken with anything gathered in the wild. The scientific name for watercress is *Nasturtium officianale,* from the Latin 'nase-tortium' which means 'nose twisting', a reference to the effect of its taste on our sniffers.

Throwing Light on Bulbs

Bulbs are a funny sort of leafy vegetable as they have leaves filled with carbohydrate to give the plant a kick start in spring, so that it can get up and flowering before the other plants choke it out. As a result of the need to store energy, bulbs contain a lot more carbohydrate (about 5 per cent) than other leafy vegetables, as well as the usual vitamins and minerals, and hardly any fat. Onions would, therefore, be highly nutritious were it not for the irresistible urge that most chefs have to fry them in fat until they are black and greasy. Spring onions are simply young onions forced for their stalks. Garlic is another widely eaten bulb which, if you believe the mystics, is a cure-all for all our ills and inadequacies.

Raw Vegetables

The benefits of raw vegetables cannot be stressed too strongly, simply because devouring them raw captures the vitamins and minerals before they are depleted by cooking. This myth that a cooked meal is always in some way superior to a cold one still persists despite the damage that cooking can cause. If you cook for Mr Fat-Tooth, a good way of persuading him to eat raw goodies is to provide a dish full of sliced or grated carrot, apples, peppers, cucumber, lettuce, cabbage, water cress, celery, tomatoes, whatever is available, on the dinner table to tuck into while they he is waiting for his main meal. That will ensure a good daily intake of beta-carotene, vitamin C and other vitamins and minerals.

Pick up a Pepper

Sweet peppers are really fruits as they have seeds in them, but they tend to be displayed amongst the vegetables. Sweet peppers, whether you call them a fruit or a vegetable, are a very rich source of both vitamin A and vitamin C. They can be eaten raw on a sandwich or in salads, and boiled or fried to form part of a variety of recipes. Green peppers are simply the unripe form of the yellow and red peppers. Peppers are very easy to grow in the greenhouse or conservatory, much easier than tomatoes as they are not so thirsty and less likely to keel over if you go away for the weekend and leave them without their usual love and attention. They are a good talking point, guaranteed to impress the neighbours, and it is surprising that they are not grown more often. If you grow their close relatives the chilli peppers be careful as the seeds of freshly picked peppers are incredibly hot. Just touching the seeds with your teeth will give you an experience far more powerful than anything you have ever experienced in an oriental restaurant. Water is no good for cooling the burn; chew on some bread or a banana instead.

Curvy Cucumbers

A salad sandwich just wouldn't be the same without a few slices of cucumber. The cucumber, that essential component of two quaint old English and American traditions – tea on the lawn, and hamburgers, respectively. (Why is it called a hamburger when it is made out of beef?). Did you know that scientists have now succeeded in growing cucumbers suitable for pickling that are big enough for one slice to cover an average hamburger. Known as the hamburger stacker it is sixteen inches long and three inches in diameter. The super cucumber was developed by a company called Vlastic International, a spin-off from Campbell Soups, in a four-year operation code named Project Frisbee. Giant pickles apparently have a big profit potential (try saying that when you're under the influence), and the company estimates that they could generate profits of at least $20 million annually.

Finger on the Pulse – Peas and Beans

Most supermarkets have a very limited selection of fresh pulses – the collective term for peas and beans – but this deficiency is more than compensated for by the abundance of dried and frozen pulses. Aduki beans, black-eyed beans, broad beans, haricot beans, lentils, butter beans, cannellini beans, chick peas, mung beans, peas and yellow split peas are all readily available in supermarkets – either dried or ready to use in tins and mixes.

Whether fresh, dried, frozen, canned or processed, peas and beans are something we should be eating more of. There is a quaint old English tradition, often remarked upon by visitors to these shores, that says you should eat peas by first getting them to stick on the back of your fork and by then attempting to raise the fork to your mouth without them falling off. This requires great skill and perseverance. Personally, I use the fork as a shovel, or preferably a spoon; it's quicker.

The Magic Mixture

Now for the magic mixture. Mix the protein in peas/beans with the protein in cereals and the result is top quality protein better than either eaten alone, and containing all of the amino acids – the protein building blocks – that we need to make the protein in our own bodies. Pulse protein + cereal protein = the perfect combination.

Proteins are made up of 20 different kinds of amino acids linked together side by side in a chain. Imagine a necklace made up of 20 differently shaped beads folded up in the palm of your hand and you will have a working idea of what a protein looks like. What makes one protein different from another is the number of each kind of amino acid (the beads) they contain and the order in which they are arranged along the chain.

The protein in red meat, fish, poultry, milk and milk products and egg whites supplies all of the amino acids we need to make the protein in our own bodies, for building muscles and making enzymes etc. Nutritionists refer to it as first-class protein. The protein in cereal grains, however, tends to lack one of the amino acids, as a result of which we would not be able to stay healthy indefinitely if cereals were the only source of our protein. The protein in most peas and beans also lacks an amino acid, but as luck would have it, it is a different amino acid from that lacking in cereals. I say 'most' peas and beans because soya beans have a more balanced amino acid content.

Mix and Match

The good news then is that cereal proteins contain plenty of the amino acid missing from peas/beans, and pea/bean proteins contain plenty of the amino acid missing from cereals, so by simply mixing the two together we can obtain all of the amino acids we need. Cereals and peas/beans are what I call the magic mixture. If you look at the label on a typical loaf of supermarket bread you will find that it is made from wheat flour that has been supplemented with soya bean flour in recognition of this fact.

Vegetarians should ideally eat cereals and pulses at the same meal, but if you can't manage that, you can have cereals for breakfast, balanced with peas and beans or other vegetables for dinner. Alternatively, just adding semi-skimmed milk to our cereal will have a similar effect, with the amino acid, lysine, in the milk proteins making up for the lack of it in the cereals.

Vegetarians have long known that the secret of staying healthy on a vegetarian diet is to eat as wide a range of food as possible, which is equally good advice whatever our eating pattern.

Bean Sprouts – Something to Shout About

Getting back to the beans though, I like all kinds but my favourites are bean sprouts. The Chinese are very fond of their bean sprouts as Chinese restaurant fans will need no reminding, and with good reason. They are rich in vitamins and easily digested protein and, what is more, are absolutely delicious and very cheap to prepare.

Preparing bean sprouts is simplicity itself. Buy the mung or adjuki beans from a supermarket or whole food store. Back at the ranch, take a couple of handfuls of the beans, rinse in cold water, then soak overnight in tepid water. Next morning, rinse again and drain off any excess water. Place several layers of paper towelling (the unbleached kind made with recycled paper is ideal) over the bottom of a shallow tray, dampen the paper thoroughly, pour off excess water, and sprinkle the beans over the surface. Cover the tray with a plastic bag and place it in a completely dark, warm spot such as an airing cupboard. Inspect occasionally to make sure that the paper remains damp but don't allow any free water to lie at the base of the tray. After about three days, remove the tray and place it in a brightly lit spot for a day or two until the sprouts turn green. Give them a rinse and they are ready to eat, either on their own or mixed with other vegetables or in salads.

Beans are not the only seeds that can be sprouted. Alfafa, a kind of grass, is another favourite with the flavour of fresh garden peas. Then there is fenugreek, radish and the familiar mustard and cress. These five can be sprouted in the dark at room temperature without extra heat. See what is available in your supermarket or health food store, but **don't** experiment with just any seed. Eat only the sprouts of seeds that are sold specifically for sprouting as others may be poisonous.

Frozen Vegetables: as Good as Fresh and Twice as Convenient

As well as iceberg lettuces, most supermarkets also have a long convoy of freezers loaded with packets of deep frozen vegetables. The packets have an embarrassing habit of tearing and releasing their contents when you pick them up to read the label.

Note that the Government reports, in recommending that as a nation we should eat more vegetables, do not differentiate between fresh and frozen. That is not an oversight on behalf of the authors. Frozen vegetables are every bit as good nutritionally as fresh, because freezing vegetables when they are still fresh traps the vitamins and prevents the levels falling significantly until they are thawed out and cooked. The freezing is done very rapidly. In one process for freezing green beans, the beans in a tunnel are exposed to a 30mph blast of cold air at −40 degrees centigrade for a few minutes. Brrh! V-v-v-vegetables f-f-frozen by such m-methods really are 'as f-fresh as w-when the p-pod w-went p-pop'.

Manufacturers sometimes add salt to their frozen vegetables, so don't forget to check the labels on the packets for the low salt brands, but mind you don't get frostbitten fingers in the process.

Frozen vegetables are one convenience food that I can heartily recommend. Such a mouth-watering variety to choose from. Indeed, we can obtain an interesting mixture such as peas, beans, and sweet corn from a single packet. Frozen vegetables are so convenient: no preparation necessary. Just snip open the packet, pop the vegetables into a pan of boiling water and zap, a few minutes later, there are the peas, beans, Brussels sprouts or whatever ready to eat.

Aspiring Mr and Mrs Trim-Guy are likely to be put off eating fresh peas, beans and Brussels sprouts on account of the time and effort involved in their preparation. This is such a pity because, despite being so fiddly to prepare, they are amongst the most nutritious of foods. Peas and beans are an excellent source of insoluble fibre to keep our bowels moving and soluble fibre to keep our cholesterol levels down. Just as importantly, eaten along with cereals, the magic mixture supplies first-class protein. Good to know then that with frozen vegetables all of the hard work has been done for us and lazy souls like myself can enjoy all of the goodness that vegetables and peas and beans have to offer. Three cheers for the frozen veg processors! Pop, Pop, Hurray! Pop, Pop, Hurray! Pop, Pop, Hurray!

The value of frozen vegetables can not be overemphasised. They are as good as fresh. They contain the same vitamins and minerals, are inexpensive, and so incredibly easy to prepare that there is absolutely no excuse for not eating more of them.

Can Canned Vegetables be as Good as Fresh?

Even canned vegetables are not to be scoffed at, so long as they aren't drowned in salt and sugar – so always read that label. Many manufacturers now provide us with the option of buying a healthy variation of their original product with less salt and sugar. Healthy and mediocre options are usually to be found sitting side by side on the same shelf, often at exactly the same price.

Read the label on some cans of baked beans and see how they differ. The table below compares three typical brands of baked beans such as you would expect to meet in your local supermarket. Each brand is available both as a healthier option low in salt and sugar and as a standard option high in salt and sugar. First, cast your eyes down the salt column. Not a lot to choose between the three brands is there? All three healthy options have the amount of salt nearly halved. Now move along to the right to the sugar column. The healthy options have less added sugar, but this time, exactly how much less varies considerably between brands. Brand C's healthy option contains

Brand	Salt: grams in 100g	Sugar: grams in 100g	Artificial Sweetener	Calories: Kcal in 100g
Brand A, ordinary	0.5	6.0	None	96
Brand A, healthy option	0.3	3.5	Saccharin	84
Brand B, ordinary	0.5	6.1	None	85
Brand B, healthy option	0.3	1.7	Acesulfame K	65
Brand C, ordinary	0.5	6.0	None	75
Brand C, healthy option	0.3	0.7	Saccharin	56

only one fifth as much sugar as Brand A's healthy option. It also contains a third less calories.

The trouble is, as usual, low sugar inexplicably means added artificial sweetener. If you want to avoid both added sugar and artificial sweeteners, tough luck! As they take away the sugar with one hand, manufacturers insist on adding artificial sweeteners with the other.

As everyone accepts that most of us consume too much salt, definitely go for the low salt options. Whether you want to go further and choose the brands with the lowest amount of sugar depends on the extent of your aversion to added sugar and how keenly you are watching the calories. If you are keen, produce a little table like the one above for other products you buy regularly. Focus on one product a week, record in a notebook the vital statistics of the different brands on offer at your local grocery store and select which is best for you. Then the next time you go shopping you can just make a beeline for the favoured brand.

If you want to make the comparison in the comfort of your own home, do as I did and buy all six cans, or however many varieties there are of the product under scrutiny. Do this just once and compare the taste as well. Sounds like a lot of work, does it, then divide the task up amongst your friends. Form a Healthy Option Club, which meets for coffee (or preferably pure orange juice) once a week for a chat and to exchange notes!

To recap then, as a general rule fresh vegetables taste the best, but frozen vegetables are as good nutritionally, and dried and canned worth keeping as a back-up for times when you can't get out to the supermarket to buy fresh or frozen.

Garden Vegetables versus Supermarket Vegetables

If you are a keen gardener, you will no doubt maintain that the vegetables you grow in your own garden taste better than those you buy in the supermarket. Are you right, or is it just a load of cow dung?

Let there be no mistake, supermarket vegetables are excellent and we should be eating more of them, but the vegetables we grow in our own garden, if we are lucky enough to have a garden, can be even better. There are two main nutritional advantages of home-grown vegetables, both relating to vitamin levels.

We can pluck our vegetables from the garden while they are young and tender, when vitamin levels are at their highest, whereas, by the time they are harvested commercially, the levels will have fallen somewhat. Secondly, we can eat the vegetables within minutes of picking while all of the vitamins are still there. Supermarket vegetables and greens still have as much protein and carbohydrate as they had when first harvested, but not so vitamin levels; they start falling slowly after harvesting and continue to do so on the supermarket shelf, so the sooner we can get our teeth into them the better. Frozen vegetables, however, keep their original vitamin levels longer.

Cultivating the Taste

But you and I eat for pleasure as well as nutrition, so another reason for growing a few cherished vegetables of our own is that they typically taste better. Why is that? Apart from being able to pick them when they are young and tender, one of the main reasons is that they contain sugar which, after they are picked, changes into starch. This is especially noticeable with sweetcorn: it really is as sweet as its name suggests when first picked, but within minutes the taste starts to suffer as enzymes convert the sugar into starch.

It takes a lot to beat the taste of a fresh young carrot, still warm from the soil. Get a good seed catalogue such as the well-known Thompson and Morgan's for advice on which vegetable varieties taste the best raw. Most root vegetables, including potatoes, taste good raw if harvested while still young and tender, but most of the more mature supermarket root vegetables need cooking to make them more palatable.

Another reason for the better taste is that when we grow vegetables in our own garden or allotment we are free to choose which varieties to grow. We can, if we wish, go for the variety that appeals most to the palate, even though it might not be the highest yielding. Farmers, on the other hand, being profit motivated, will opt for the higher yielding variety or the one most resistant to pests, even if it wins no prizes for taste.

The only trouble with growing your own vegetables is that it involves a fair amount of work, especially if you have to dig up a dense grassy patch to get started. Here's a tip for any readers who expect to be spending a spell inside in the near future. First, get your wife to write you a letter in prison saying, 'I have decided to plant some cabbages in the back garden. When is the best time to plant them?' Now, you know that the prison guards will read all of the mail so you reply, 'Dear wife, whatever you do, don't touch the back garden. That is where I hid all of the jewellery.' A week or so later you will receive another letter from your wife, 'You wouldn't believe what happened, some men came to the house with shovels and dug up all the back garden.' Then you can write another letter. 'Dear wife, now is the best time to plant the cabbage.'

To be serious again, the last thing I want to do is to put anyone off buying supermarket vegetables. Even with their generally poorer taste and slightly lower vitamin levels, they are still nutritionally one of the best foods around, packed with carbohydrate and protein, fibre, vitamins and minerals and much, much more. Remember the official advice that nationally our consumption of fresh and frozen vegetables should double. It's good advice and we should stick to it whether the vegetables come from the supermarket, the local greengrocer's or our own treasured vegetable plots or window boxes.

Chapter 4

Two-Headed Cabbages –
Genetically Modified Foods

Traditional methods of plant breeding involve transferring genetic material between plants of the same species. Starting with, for instance, a wild variety of a potato that is resistant to a certain kind of virus, you cross it with a crop variety which is not in an effort to create plants with all the desirable characteristics of the commercial variety together with the virus resistance from the wild variety. This is very much a hit or miss affair, as the vast majority of crosses will inherit undesirable characteristics from the wild variety as well as the virus resistance. It's a bit like expecting your children to inherit all of your spouse's good characteristics without any of the bad. Traditional plant breeding is also very time-consuming; it can take ten years just to change the petal colour of a flower. Now, armed with the latest tools of genetic engineering, scientists can identify the genes responsible for traits such as disease resistance and transfer them from one species to another to produce hardier or more productive crops.

How Do They Do That?

Let us suppose that the genetic engineers wish to transfer a desirable foreign gene for, say, disease resistance, that they have isolated from, say, a wild variety of potato, into a susceptible commercial variety. At this point the genetic engineers will work not with the whole plant but with individual plant cells growing in culture. Using one of a variety of techniques, they insert the foreign gene into the cells. Only a tiny proportion of the plant cells will take on board the foreign gene, however, and it will take six months to a year to regenerate the cells into complete plants to find out which did so. To speed things up, therefore, the genetic engineers attach a marker gene to the foreign gene. This marker gene contains the information for destroying the antibiotics, kanamycin and neomycin. The engineers then add the antibiotic to the mixture of cells. Most are killed, but those that have taken on board the desirable gene with its attached anti-antibiotic destroy the antibiotic and survive. That's why, as we shall see later, some genetically engineered foods contain anti-antibiotics.

Is Genetically Modified Food Safe?

That's a bit like asking if food is safe to eat. Scientists can modify food genetically in many different ways. In many cases, it is hard to see how the modification – like shortening a gene that is already present in a tomato to prevent it going soft so quickly on ripening – could possibly do anyone any harm. There is nothing intrinsically harmful about genetically modified food. It is exactly what is inserted into the new plant that is important. Does it now produce an insecticide that in large amounts could be harmful to some people who eat it, for example? But then, any new variety of a fruit or vegetable could turn out to produce something unpleasant in larger amounts than previously. There is hardly any natural food, plant or animal that someone isn't allergic to. Millions of people throughout the world cannot drink cows' milk, either due to an allergy to its proteins or because their intestines are unable to handle the milk sugar it contains. There are people who are allergic to peanuts, broad beans, tomatoes, you name it, someone will be allergic to it. Eating is a dangerous game. But not nearly so dangerous as not eating. We consume small amounts of many toxic substances every day, but our bodies can handle them. It is when certain additives or plant products start appearing everywhere – like artificial sweeteners – that we have to start to worry about whether the body's detoxification system might be overloaded.

With proper regulation, there is no reason why genetically modified foods cannot be produced which are as safe as normal foods.

Genetically Modified Foods and the Environment

In common with most scientific advances, genetic engineering can be exploited for good or evil, and its effects on the environment can be either. On the one hand it might cut down the use of insecticides or reduce waste, but on the other increase the use of herbicides or allow habitats previously unsuitable for growing crops to be exploited to the detriment of wildlife. Let's see how.

Arming Crops against Their Enemies

Many plants produce their own insecticides as a defence against the insects from which they are under constant attack. A familiar example is pyrethrum, an insecticide extracted from a kind of chrysanthemum, which many of us use in our own gardens. The ability to insert the genetic information for producing insecticides into crops that don't have any of their own would at first sight seem to be an environmental blessing. No longer would it be necessary to spray fields with insecticides, killing friend and foes indiscriminately. Only those armies of insects that attacked the crops would be killed, leaving the innocent civilians that confined themselves to the weeds unharmed. This is good news for the insects and good news for the birds and other wild life that feed on the insects.

The arming of previously defenceless crops with insecticides by genetic engineering has been achieved, and potatoes and maize containing their own insecticides are already on the market. The maize insecticide makes the crop resistant to the European corn-borer, a serious agricultural pest. This particular insecticide did not come from another species of plant, but from a bacterium called Bt. Nothing to do with British Telecom. The Bt in this case stands for *Bacillus thuringiensis*. Some kinds of insects, like threadworms, actually make a meal of bacteria, so it makes sense for the bacterial victims to fight back by producing insecticides. Powdered preparations of Bt and its insecticide have long been used as a natural insecticide for spraying on crops. Genetic engineers have now succeeded in isolating the genetic information for making the insecticide from the bacteria and inserted it into potatoes, maize and other crops. The insecticide is broken down in our stomachs and, as far as is known, doesn't do us any harm, but don't feed genetically modified crops to your pet stick insects!

This will be an environmental blessing only, of course, so long as the inbuilt insecticide really is replacing sprayed insecticide and not introducing one into fields where none was used previously. Nothing is ever as straightforward as it seems at first sight.

Strains of insect resistant to the inbuilt insecticide will inevitably emerge eventually, just as we find insects, fungi and other pests developing resistance to sprayed insecticides etc.

Fear has also been expressed that the insecticide gene might somehow find its way from the crop into a weed, giving rise to a superweed which, freed of the natural control conferred by insects, would take over, choking out neighbouring weeds and causing serious environmental damage. This regularly happens when foreign weeds are introduced into countries where the particular species of insects and other creatures that, in their homeland, keep them under control are absent.

Then there is the fear that bee populations gathering nectar from the flowers of, for instance, genetically modified rape, might be wiped out. As many plants, both wild and commercial, depend on insects such as bees for their pollination the potential for disaster is obvious.

Environmentally Unfriendly Herbicide Resistance

Definitely without any pretensions to environmental friendliness is the insertion of herbicide resistance into plants. Often a weedkiller cannot be used on a particular crop because it kills the crop as well as the weeds. One answer is to insert a gene into the crop that makes it resistant to a particular herbicide so that the fields can be sprayed to kill the weeds without killing the crop. Sounds like an environmental disaster that one – less wild flowers, more herbicide residues contaminating our food, and in poorer countries a lot of unemployed farm labourers. It is all the more worrying when a company that produces the herbicide is at the forefront of the development of crops resistant to it. Monsanto is one such company that has engineered soya and is proceeding with a range of other genetically modified crops designed to be resistant to Round Up, a herbicide manufactured by the same company that currently generates annual revenues of close on a billion pounds. Extending the use of the herbicide to crops with the herbicide-resistant gene will cause profits to soar even higher.

Tastier Tomatoes

The first genetically modified tomatoes made their appearance on the supermarket shelves in the USA in 1994 and in the UK in 1996. One type of genetically modified tomato contains a gene, known as the Flavr Savr gene, which causes them to soften more slowly during ripening than traditional tomatoes. This means that the grower can wait until the fruit has fully ripened before harvesting it, thus ending up with an improved flavour, hence the name of the gene. As if 'Lite' were not bad enough, 'Flavr Savr', what next! This piece of genetic engineering means less wastage and, as the tomatoes contain less water, less energy is used during processing. Sounds like a good thing environmentally and for the tomato gourmet. Any problems?

One annoying little hitch is that in developing the genetically modified tomato, the gene with the information for producing the protein which destroys the antibiotics kanomycin and neomycin was attached to the Flavr Savr gene to help identify those tomato cells that had taken it on board. When we eat tomatoes it is theoretically possible that this anti-antibiotic gene, if not destroyed by cooking, might jump ship from the tomatoes into bacteria resident in our intestines, resulting in strains of bacteria

resistant to the two antibiotics. These resistant strains might then spread across the nation, rendering these two particular antibiotics ineffective in treating certain bacterial infections. A theoretical possibility yes, but then what disaster isn't theoretically possible.

The good news is that alternative and seemingly harmless marker genes are now available and we can expect these to rapidly replace the anti-antibiotic markers in new products that are developed in the future.

Designer Everything

The potato, that close relative of the tomato, is also a major target crop for genetic modification. There are a great many reasons for producing genetically modified potatoes: for resistance to viruses, nematodes and fungi, for improved storage and processing. How long will it be before a potato x tomato hybrid thrusts itself on our attention, spuds underground, tomatoes on top, developed by a combination of traditional means and genetic engineering.

There is potentially an endless variety of traits that can be genetically engineered into plants: drought and salt resistance, improved nutritional content, improved storage and processing, flavour etc. Each would have its own environmental implications, some good, some bad. Not all genetically modified plants will find their way onto the food shelves. Cotton and tobacco, for example, are prime candidates for genetic modification to protect them from pests. In the case of tobacco, may the pests reign supreme!

Animal-Plant Hybrids

Not quite the all-dancing, all-singing fruit and vegetables of the TV ads. What we are contemplating is the insertion into a plant of a small piece of DNA from an animal that causes the plant to produce a particular animal protein. One of the main reasons for attempting to incorporate animal proteins into plants would be to improve the nutritional value of their proteins. Nevertheless, inserting animal genes into plants does raise important ethical issues that need to be addressed. Would a genetically modified vegetable containing a gene originally derived from pigs be unsuitable for Muslims, or a gene from any animal be unsuitable for vegetarians. Could eating human proteins produced by plants be regarded as cannibalism?

Meaningful Labelling

Food producers and retailers are required to label all genetically modified foods as such to give consumers a choice. In my view a simple label that a product is genetically engineered is not going far enough. It is just like saying that a product contains an additive. What additive? Vitamin C, tartrazine or what? In the case of genetically modified food, we want to know what the food is modified with. Does it contain Bt insecticide plus anti-antibiotic, a herbicide resistance gene or what? Those concerned about the environment might well find the insecticide acceptable (depending on the size of the threat to bees and other beneficial or rare insects etc) but not the herbicide resistance, and they would need this information to help them make up their mind whether to buy the product.

It is one thing, however, to have a genetically modified tomato which is clearly labelled so that we have a clear choice between can A and can B, but soya and maize pose a much bigger problem. They are added to such a wide range of processed foods that they are becoming increasingly untraceable, so we don't know if we are eating them or not. Ingredients like lecithin and oils derived from genetically modified plants are even more difficult to track through the food chain. This is far from being an acceptable situation.

Genetically Modified Dairy Produce

Not only plants are genetically modified. Rennet, used in cheese making to cause the cheese to clot, has long posed a problem for vegetarians, because it comes from calf intestines. A substance called chymosin, produced by a genetically engineered micro-organism, has been developed to replace rennet and is now widely used in the cheese industry in the USA and some European countries, including Britain, particularly in vegetarian cheeses.

Over to You

So there are some facts to ponder. The final decision is yours. If we are to make an intelligent choice and not tar all genetically modified foods with the same brush, I think everyone will agree that effective labelling and more factual information are essential.

Chapter 5

Vital Vitamins and Mighty Minerals

Bottled Vitamins

What's this? A shelf full of bottles of vitamin pills in a store brimming over with fresh food. Shouldn't a good, varied diet already contain all of the vitamins we need? Indeed it should, but there is probably no harm in taking extra vitamin pills occasionally or a vitamin-rich extract like cod liver oil, with its vitamins A, D and E, just to make sure, so long as we don't overdo them. If you are a vegetarian your intake of vitamin D and vitamin B12 could be on the low side, so a supplement of these may be worth considering. If you do take extra vitamins, take care never to exceed the amount recommended by the manufacturers on the bottle and always remember that a bottle containing a few purified vitamins is no substitute for the nutritional complexity of a healthy varied diet.

In our expedition to the greengrocers we were keen to extol the virtues of foods rich in vitamin C and beta-carotene (which our bodies convert into vitamin A). Let us now meet some other key vitamins and remind ourselves what they are, why we need them and where they come from. To help us remember we will organise the vitamins into groups.

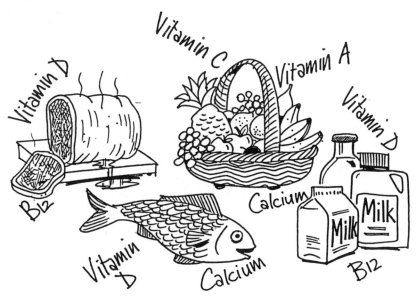

Vitamins A, C and E, they're ACE

In our first group we have vitamins A, C and E. This spells ACE, so we can call them the ACE vitamins. Why not? This nemomic, or mnemonic rather, (why is mnemonic such a difficult word to remember how to spell?) is a silly but convenient way of remembering that these three vitamins have something important in common. They all act as antioxidants, substances that interact in the body with damaging chemicals known as free radicals, rendering them harmless. Evidence is accumulating that the ACE vitamins and other free radical busters may help to protect against the sort of damage to the cells in your body which may eventually lead to certain forms of cancer and heart disease. You may have noticed this word 'antioxidant' on the labels of processed foods, especially those containing fats such as powdered milk. The purpose of adding antioxidants is to prevent them from deteriorating. The antioxidant used is often vitamin C, usually addressed when occupying this role by its formal scientific title of L-ascorbic acid.

Sources of ready-made Vitamin A

Animal products only	Micrograms of Vitamin A in each 100 grams (3.5 ounces) of food.
Calf liver	30,000
Lamb, ox and pig liver	16,000 to 20,000
Chicken liver	11,000
Liver pate	7,300
Liver sausage	2,600
Haggis	1,800
Faggots	460
Cod liver oil	18,000 (about 900 in a 5ml teaspoon)
Eggs and egg products	
Whole, raw chicken eggs	190 (about 2 grade 6 eggs) All in the yolk
Whole, raw duck eggs	540
Omelette and quiche	Around 200
Gateau	Around 250
Milk and dairy products	
Full-fat milk	50 (about 300 in a pint)
Semi skimmed milk	20 (about 120 in a pint)
Skimmed milk	1 (hardly any)
Butter	820
Low-fat spread	920
Double cream	600
Cheese, Cheddar	330
Dairy vanilla ice cream	120
Margarine	780

Open Your Eyes to Vitamin A

As well as serving as a free radical-busting antioxidant, vitamin A, as we revealed in extolling the virtues of carrots, also has a night job. It helps us to see in the dark. It is also essential for the eyes in a different way. In many poorer parts of the world, a severe lack of the vitamin in the diet is one of the main causes of blindness.

Ready-made vitamin A is a constituent of fish oils and dairy produce but, as can be seen from the table below, by far the biggest source is liver. A mouthful of liver will keep us going for weeks. This includes chicken liver. That little plastic bag of giblets which comes hidden inside the chicken is an excellent source of vitamin A, not to mention vitamin B12 and iron, so don't always bin it.

A word of warning. If you take supplements of vitamin A, never exceed the stated dose as it is toxic in large amounts. This was discovered to their cost by the early Arctic explorers. They knew that the native Eskimos never ate the liver of the polar bears they hunted but thought they were just being silly, so they went ahead and tucked into it. As a result, they became violently ill, the reason being that polar bear liver contains enormous mounts of vitamin A on account, no doubt, of all of the oily fish they eat. Also as polar bears often have to go without food for months at a time, it makes sense for them to stockpile as much as possible. So when you are next in your local supermarket be sure to steer clear of the polar bear liver! The more familiar kinds of liver are good for us in moderation most of the time but, owing to its high vitamin A content, the current medical advice it that liver should be avoided during pregnancy or at least eaten then in only very small amounts. That is, avoided by expectant mothers; expectant fathers can carry on eating it.

If you are a vegetarian there is no need to worry about vitamin A as it is not essential to consume the ready-made vitamin. We are all DIY experts capable of knocking it together ourselves with our biochemical tool kit from the beta-carotene found in all dark green leafy vegetables and in root vegetables, especially carrots. Cereals typically contain very little beta-carotene, but sweet corn is yellowish – a real giveaway – and, sure enough, has significant amounts.

Vitamin A or its precursor beta-carotene occur in such a wide variety of products that there is little need to go actively searching for it. It will find us! Eat lots of fresh vegetables along with just a little fat or oil to help your intestines to absorb the beta-carotene, and you will not go short.

Sources of ready-made Vitamin A are shown in the table. The Recommended Daily Amount (RDA) is 800 micrograms. The beta-carotene precursor is found in all fruit and vegetables, the richest sources being carrots and peppers and dark, leafy vegetables, especially curly kale.

Everyone's Favourite: Vitamin C

Like vitamin A, vitamin C is a free radical-buster, exploiting its antioxidant properties to mop up free radicals and protect, so the optimistic postulate, against certain kinds of cancer. Clinical trials are currently under way to determine whether large doses of the vitamin can help to prevent what are known as pre-cancerous lesions, that is changes in the stomach wall with an increased risk of developing into cancer, from actually doing so. It is too early to say yet whether there is anything in the idea.

In our voyage of discovery through the fruit-laden shelves of the greengrocers we remarked about James Lind's recognition of the anti-scurvy properties of lemons and limes. It was not until the early 1930s, a century and a half later, that the fruits' remark-

Where to aim your trolley for Vitamin C

Sources	Milligrams of Vitamin C in each 100g (3.5 ounces) of food
Veggie Vitamin C	
Red peppers	140
Green peppers	120
Brussels sprouts, fresh or frozen	120
Curly kale	110
Broccoli	90
Cabbage	50
Cauliflower	40
Mange tout peas	50
Other peas	20
Parsnips	20
New potatoes	20 (modest levels but we eat a lot)
Old potatoes	10 (freshly dug contain about 21 mg)
Tomatoes	20
Parsley	190 (high levels but we tend to eat very small amounts)
Watercress	60
Most other vegetables	10-30
Fruitie vitamin C	
Blackcurrants	200
Strawberries	80
Lemons	60
Oranges, Clementines	50
Lychees	40
Grapefruit	40
Canteloupe melon	30
Raspberries	30
Apples	2 to 20 (depending on variety)
Most other fruit	10 to 20
Jam	10
Fruit pies and canned fruit	Wide variation in amounts
Fruit Juices	
Pure orange juice	20
Ribena blackcurrant fruit juice drink	30 – a small glass (200ml) provides the EC, RDA
Five Alive fruit juice drink	10
(Most squashes and other non-pure fruit juices are fortified with Vitamin C)	
Less obvious sources	
Processed potatoes	
Frozen chips	20
Instant powdered potatoes	20 fortified
Crisps	30
A few breakfast cereals	(Not normally present in cereals)
Bran flakes	50 fortified
Weetos	30 fortified
Fortified milk	(Only small amounts normally present in milk)
UHT milk	30
Dried skimmed milk	10
Bread	Used as an improving agent in flour

able properties could be attributed to their high vitamin C content. It was not only adventurous seafarers deprived of fresh fruit and vegetables who suffered from scurvy in times past, but ordinary townsfolk too. Mediaeval portraits depict the skin sores characteristic of the disease. People living in northern areas would have been especially susceptible after a cold, damp spell when fresh fruit supplies were limited. Today, at the start of the twenty-first century, few people in the UK consume so little vitamin C that they come down with the severest forms of scurvy rife in mediaeval times. A few, however, typically as a result of self neglect due, for instance, to chronic alcoholism, still manage to consume such small amounts as to render themselves susceptible to internal bruising, poor healing of wounds and bleeding gums. Many people believe from personal experience that vitamin C helps to prevent them from catching colds, but it has proven surprisingly difficult to prove this scientifically.

The annoying thing about vitamin C is that we need a regular daily supply as, unlike vitamin A, we lack a storage depot for it in our bodies. This is no problem to those of us who eat fresh fruit and vegetables and drink pure fruit juices daily, but people on a junk food diet may be struggling to get enough. Puzzling though, isn't it, how some people we know seem to consume hardly any of the fresh fruit and vegetables that contain vitamin C, and yet escape the scurvy our ancestors used to be prone to. The only logical explanation for this, unless they are so embarrassed to be caught eating healthily that they do it at night in the secrecy of their own homes, is that they consume hidden vitamin C. By 'hidden vitamin C' I mean the L-ascorbic acid - vitamin C by just another name - that manufacturers add to a variety of processed foods such as bread, tinned fruit, fizzy drinks, powdered potatoes and powdered milk. Occasionally they add it to their products to replace the naturally occurring vitamin that has been lost in processing, but as often as not its purpose is to act as an antioxidant to prevent fats going off.

How much vitamin C should we consume in a day? Sixty milligrams is the recommended amount in the UK, 100mg in the USA. It's not that Americans need more vitamin C than UK folk, but rather that scientific opinion differs. If you are a mathematical genius and carry a pair of kitchen scales around with you, you will be able to work out how much of what food to eat to get this amount. If not, I have a simpler solution – just drink a glass of pure orange juice a day. A medium-sized glass holding 300ml gives us the 60mg we need, painlessly. Then eat whatever fresh fruit you can get your hands on.

If you happen to consume more than this, for instance if you have orange juice with your breakfast, broccoli or other members of the cabbage family with your main meal, and blackcurrants for a snack, you are unlikely to come to any harm, as the excess is just excreted. Unlike some other vitamins, C dissolves in water, which makes it easy to excrete any excess. Don't go over the top though; if you become a vitamin C junky and pop lots of vitamin C pills as well, you might end up with kidney stones composed of the stuff.

Limiting the Loss

The water solubility of vitamin C has its downside. When we boil vegetables, a significant amount of the vitamin leaks out into the water, so boil for as short as time as possible and in as little water as possible. Better still, keep the water and use it to make soup. "Waiter, waiter, there's a fly in my soup." "Sorry, Sir, I didn't realise you were a vegetarian."

Everyone knows how important it is to keep meat and poultry cool to prevent an invasion of food poisoning bacteria, but with the bacterial threat from fruit and vegetables being so much less, we often don't bother at what temperature we store them. Note, however, that in the days and weeks following harvesting, vegetables gradually lose their vitamin C, and the higher the temperature at which you store them, the faster they lose it. So always keep fruit and vegetables in a cool place, preferably the refrigerator, if there is room, or get a bigger one next time you need a replacement.

As we navigated our passage through the international waters of the fruit and vegetable store I pointed out many of the richest sources of vitamin C. These are summarised in the table below, but don't forget that the levels I have given are those in good quality fresh produce. As the exact amounts vary enormously between samples, they should be seen as approximate figures to give you an idea of what to expect. Store vegetables next to a radiator, or over-boil them, and vitamin levels will plummet.

Eating E is Easy

Rich sources of Vitamin A	
Sources	Milligrams of Vitamin E in each 100 grams (3.5 ounces) of food
Cod Liver Oil	100 (5 in a 5ml teaspoon)
Cooking Oils	
Wheatgerm oil	137
Sunflowerseed oil	49
Cottonseed and Safflower oil	42
Soya, Corn, Peanut and Rapeseed oil	16 to 22
Margarine: (25g, about 1oz)	8
Eggs	1 (about 0.5 in a grade 6 egg)
Nuts and Seeds (without shells)	
Sunflower seeds	38
Hazel nuts	25
Almonds	24
Peanuts	10
Brazil nuts	7
Marzipan	6
Fruit and Vegetables: A Few Examples	
Sweet potato	5
Blackberries	2
Spinach	2
Mangoes	1
Pears	0.5
High Fibre Breakfast Cereals	
All-Bran	2
Muesli Swiss style	3

In common with the other ACE vitamins, vitamin E is an antioxidant assisting our bodies in their fight against free radicals, thereby supposedly helping to protect against a whole range of diseases, including cancer and heart disease. Polyunsaturated fat gourmets have an increased need for vitamin E but, fortunately, foods high in polyunsaturates, like vegetable oils, also tend to be naturally high in the vitamin.

Where else is Vitamin E to be found? Virtually all food, whether derived from an animal or plant, has a significant amount of Vitamin E so it is just about impossible to suffer from a severe deficiency on anything other than a starvation diet. White bread and white rice are very exceptional in containing hardly any, emphasising the foolhardiness of removing the nutritious husk from cereal grains.

The table below gives an idea of where to aim your trolley for the richest sources. Note: don't consume excessive amounts of cooking oil or spread oodles of margarine specially to get vitamin E as they increase the need for it, so consuming them tends to be self-defeating.

Vitamin D – Give Me Sunshine, Give Me Fish

The second group of vitamins has but one member, vitamin D, the sunshine vitamin. It is present in full-fat milk and semi-skimmed milk (but not skimmed milk) and in milk products like half-fat cheese, as well as in fish. DIY enthusiasts will be heartened to learn that we can also make it ourselves in our skin with the help of ultraviolet light. Don't overdo the sunbathing though and watch where you do it.

It was Jim Fat-Tooth's day off and he was sunbathing naked on the roof of the hotel where he had a summer job, when the manager appeared.

"This is neither the time nor the place for nudity," he snorted.

"Why not? Nobody ever comes up here, and there is a wall all the way round the roof." replied Jim in amazement.

"I am aware of that," replied the manager, "but you are lying on the skylight over the restaurant and the guests are about to have lunch."

As we learned in our history lessons at school, in the early days of industrialisation, children in big cities like London and Glasgow often suffered from rickets, a disease characterised by failure of the bones to develop properly. The cause of this was a deficiency of vitamin D and calcium, which arose because they were not able to obtain a balanced diet containing enough of the fish, milk and dairy products that contain these nutrients. The lack of vitamin D would not have mattered had they been exposed to adequate sunshine to allow them to make it in their skin. Sadly, they lived in high rise tenements which shielded them from what little sunlight managed to penetrate the thick band of smoke emanating from the factories and coal fires, and holidays in Benidorm or Tenerife were unheard of. So, despite recent killjoy skin cancer prevention campaigns, sunshine is not all bad but, like everything else, it needs to be taken in moderation and at the right time and place.

People at Risk of a Deficiency

Vitamin D deficiency can sometimes be a problem even today for people with dark skin living in the UK or cloudier parts of the United States because it takes more sunshine to produce the vitamin in dark skin than it does in white. If, for religious reasons or because they cannot tolerate milk sugar or proteins, they are unable to eat dairy products the risk is greater. Vitamin D deficiency can also arise in people who are housebound and unable to get out in the sunshine. If you do the shopping for an elderly relative or neighbour, when possible go for the brands with vitamin D supplements.

Granny's Cure is at Hand

For those at risk of vitamin D deficiency there is, however, a good old-fashioned remedy – cod liver oil!

Don't groan too loud. You can always mix it with a yoghurt or a glass of orange juice if you don't like the taste, or alternatively invest in pots of malt extract and cod liver oil, which most folk find much tastier than the neat oil. It's good stuff, cod liver oil, packed with Vitamins A, D and E and, as if this were not enough, also with the blood-thinning Omega-3 essential fatty acids. More about the Omega-3 acids later. Topping up with cod liver oil will not be necessary if we are including plenty of salmon, trout, mackerel, sardines, tuna and other oily fish, either fresh or in cans, in

Where to Find Vitamin D on a Rainy Day.
On a Sunny Day, Just Relax in the Garden and Make Your Own!

Sources	Micrograms of Vitamin D in each 100 grams (3.5 ounces) of food
Oily Fish	
Cod liver oil	210 (10 in a 5ml teaspoon)
Herring, kipper and mackerel	Between 15 and 25
Canned salmon	13
Canned pilchards and sardines	8
White fish	Just a trace
Fortified margarine	8
Hens' Eggs	2 (ducks' eggs have twice as much)
Fortified breakfast Cereals – e.g. Corn Flakes, Coco Pops & Rice Crispies	Usually around 2.8. Read the labels
Fortified beverages – e.g. Complan, Horlics & Ovaltine	2 per 100g powder (About 0.25 made up)
Milk and Dairy Products	
Butter	0.8
Cheese	Around 0.2
Vanilla ice cream	0.1
Full-fat cows' milk	0.03
Semi skimmed cows milk	0.01
Enriched semi-skimmed cows milk.	0.03
Meat and Poultry	Just a trace
Fruit, Vegetables, Bread and Unfortified Cereals	None
Recommended Daily Amount In Winter	5.0 micrograms

our diet. Nor if we are blessed with more summers like that of '95 (but not 2000!) which enable us to get out and about in the sunshine.

Boning up on Osteoporosis

Bone is very important to us. Without it, we would be featureless blobs. Although no one ever gets quite to that state, a shortage can cause rickets in children and increase the risk of developing osteoporosis later in life. Rickets is a disease that can arise during childhood in response to a severe lack of calcium and vitamin D in the diet. Although few children and young adults in developed countries today consume so little calcium and vitamin D that they develop rickets, they may still be consuming too little to adequately protect themselves against the effects of osteoporosis in later life.

'Osteoporosis' means *porous bones*. The 'osteo' bit means *bones* and 'porosis', *porous* – doctors often speak front to back. Bones affected by osteoporosis lose much of their calcium, and develop holes like Swiss cheese. The bones of the hip, vertebrae and wrist are the most susceptible, and easily fractured following a fall. Osteoporosis is the main cause of hip fractures in the elderly, and weakening of the spinal column leads to a stooping posture and a dowager's hump. Although a condition mainly associated with women because they tend to have smaller bone structures to begin with, osteoporosis can also affect men, but usually at a more advanced age.

The amount of bone we have supporting our bodies reaches its peak at around the age of thirty, so the more we have by then the better. After 30 or so, we start to lose bone mass. By ensuring that we get enough calcium and vitamin D when we are young and by engaging in physical activity to build up strong healthy bones, we can lower our risk of developing osteoporosis later in life. For many readers of this book, this advice will come too late. Never mind, a healthy diet and plenty of exercise will still help us, if not to increase bone mass, at least to reduce the rate at which it is lost.

Vitamin D and calcium are, however, far from being the whole story in regard to osteoporosis. Many other factors are involved too, including hormones and an inherited tendency to the condition. As the level of the female hormone oestrogen declines at the menopause, bone is lost twice to four times as fast as before the menopause. This rate of loss continues for a few years, after which it slows down somewhat, but even so, by the time they reach their sixty-fifth birthday some women have lost half of their bone mass.

There are high-tech methods available nowadays of detecting osteoporosis in its early stages, and a bewildering array of treatments available aimed at slowing down the bone loss and preventing disability. These treatments are more likely to be effective if we ensure that our intake of calcium and vitamin D remains adequate throughout life.

The B Vitamins

Two of the best known of the third group of vitamins are thiamine (vitamin B1) and niacin, which help us to release the energy in our food. Small amounts are present in a wide variety of animal and plant foods. The husks of cereal grains are a good source of these vitamins; they therefore occur naturally in wholemeal bread but have to be added to white. In fortified breakfast cereals extra B vitamins are added to what are there already. A shortage of thiamine (B1) and niacin in the diet may lead to tiredness, muscle weakness, loss of appetite and nausea, but so do dozens of other things, so it's always difficult to pinpoint the precise reason for such symptoms. A very severe lack of thiamine results in a disease called beri beri once prevalent in South East Asia. The process of rice polishing, removing the outer skin of the rice in order to make white rice, was introduced in the seventeenth century, following which beri beri, a disease affecting the heart and nervous system, became widespread throughout the region. Such an extreme deficiency is unlikely to affect people in developed nations today.

Riboflavin (vitamin B2) is another vitamin that helps us to release energy from the food we eat. Much of the riboflavin in our diet comes from dairy products, such as milk, cheese and yoghurt. Don't worry if you drink only skimmed milk as there is just

In Search of the Elusive Vitamin B12

Sources	Micrograms of Vitamin B12 in each 100 grams (3.5 ounces) of food
SOURCES FOR CARNIVORES Meat	
Beef, lamb and pork	2
Rabbit	10
Duck, goose and pheasant	2 to 3
Turkey	2
Chicken, dark meat	1
Bovril	8
Fish	
Oily fish, fresh and canned	4 to 6
White fish	2
Fish fingers	2
SOURCES FOR VEGETARIANS	
Eggs	
Duck egg (all in the yolk)	5.4
Chicken egg (all in the yolk)	2.5 (about 1.9 in a 75g class 1 egg)
Milk and Dairy Produce	
Pasteurised milk, full-fat, semi-skimmed or skimmed	0.4
UHT milk	0.2
Sterilised milk	0.1
Cheeses, full-fat and reduced	1 to 2
Yoghurts	0.2
Ice-cream	0.4
SOURCES FOR VEGANS	
Marmite	0.5
Surprise sources of B12: look for others.	
Fortified fruit juice drinks	
e.g. Ribena blackcurrant juice drink	0.5
Fortified breakfast cereals:	
e.g. Coco Pops, Kellogg's Cornflakes, Frosties, Rice Crispies, Nestle Multicheerios, Nesquik, Ready Brek, Weetos	0.8 to 1.0
Heinz spaghetti hoops	0.5

as much riboflavin in skimmed milk and low-fat cheeses as in full-fat. Riboflavin is very sensitive to light, so if you buy your milk in bottles keep them in a dark spot, and if you have them delivered, don't leave them too long on the doorstep. If the thought of getting up at 5.30am every morning is too daunting, leave a lightproof box on the doorstep in summer for the milkman to conceal from the blistering rays of the morning sun. I am nothing if not optimistic! Eggs are also an egg-cellent source of riboflavin. It is not, however, exclusively an animal vitamin; fruit, vegetables and cereals will happily supply the needs of vegans. One of the first symptoms of a lack of riboflavin is an increase in susceptibility to cracks and sores about the mouth, again a pretty inconclusive sort of symptom.

Now for a brief mention of three lesser-known B vitamins: pyridoxine (vitamin B6), biotin, and pantothenic acid (vitamin B5). They are less well known because deficiencies of them are extremely rare. Pyridoxine has many functions in the body, mostly related to the proper use of proteins. It is found in a wide variety of animal and plant foods including liver, wholemeal breads, fish, nuts and fortified breakfast cereals. A deficiency can result in muscle weakness and irritability. Again, so can a lot of other things, like sitting at a word processor all day. Biotin has many roles in the body, including, once again, helping us to obtain energy from the food we eat. It is found in a wide variety of animal and plant foods.

Pantothenic acid (vitamin B5) is

also found in a wide variety of foods so again a deficiency is very unlikely to occur. It, too, helps us to release energy from food.

Give Us This Day Our Daily B

All of the above mentioned B vitamins are water-soluble and, when we consume more than we need, we excrete the excess in our urine rather than storing it. As a result, we need to eat some every day. They are found in such a wide range of foods that a serious deficiency is unlikely, but if you want to be really sure of obtaining enough, have a sandwich of a yeast extract like Marmite on wholemeal bread! Yes, yeast and wholemeal bread are two of the richest sources of B vitamins, so a daily sandwich of yeast extract will put you well on the road to your recommended daily amount! Also, for that matter, will fortified breakfast cereals which, as the labels proclaim, have Bs in abundance.

Vitamin B12, the Vegan's Nightmare

It has B in its name, but vitamin B12 is so different in many respects from the other B Vitamins that it deserves to be put in a class on its own. B12 has a different kind of function in the body, and in contrast to the other B vitamins we can store it in our liver, so we don't need to consume it every day. Also, unlike the other B vitamins, it does not occur naturally in fruit, vegetables or cereals. B12 is often found hanging around with the other B vitamins in packets of breakfast cereal, but only because it has been introduced by the manufacturers.

Being absent from fruit, vegetables and cereals, vitamin B12 is the vegan's nightmare. Is there then no natural source from which they can obtain it without committing the ultimate sin of consuming animal products? Fortunately, B12 is also found in yeast and seaweed, which can be eaten directly, or it can be extracted and provided in pill form. A sigh of relief!

An inadequate intake of vitamin B12 results in pernicious anaemia, a type of anaemia fairly common in older people. In most victims, however, the illness is due not so much to a lack of the vitamin in the diet as to a difficulty of absorbing it from the intestines, a failing that commonly arises in later life. If popping B12 pills or eating liver, the richest of sources, doesn't do the trick, the vitamin has to be injected directly into the blood.

Because of the limited range of foods in which B12 occurs and because we are unable to make it ourselves in our own bodies, vegans (who avoid not only meat and fish but also dairy products and eggs) are at great risk of a deficiency. Vegans need to take positive steps to ensure that they are getting enough, and most now recognise the need for supplements. Vegetarians who consume dairy products and egg yolks are at less risk of a deficiency. B12 is, however, required in incredibly small amounts. The daily recommended intake is just one millionth of a gram (1 microgram), so a kilogram bag would provide you with enough to last a thousand, million days!

When we consume more vitamin B12 than we can make use of immediately, we store the excess in our livers. Consequently, most of us have enough stockpiled to keep us going for months even if our diet suddenly became so inadequate that it supplied us with none at all. It is becoming increasingly difficult to suffer from a deficiency of vitamin B12 as it keeps turning up in unexpected places as a supplement. Manufacturers add it to a variety of products that do not contain it naturally, including some breakfast cereals, fruit drinks, even cans of spaghetti rings!

Folic Acid: Find it in Foliage

Folic acid, as its name suggests (foliage), is found in green leafy vegetables, although it is by no means confined to them. Potatoes and oranges are also useful sources. An adequate intake is particularly important during early pregnancy, as there is evidence to suggest that a deficiency may increase the risk of spina bifida in the offspring. Doctors often automatically provide pregnant women with supplements on the assumption that they cannot be trusted to eat their greens.

Mining for Minerals: Calcium

As well as our industry, our bodies are also dependent on a ready supply of a wide variety of minerals.

By far the most abundant mineral in our bodies is calcium, 99 per cent of it in our bones and teeth. Tiny amounts are also needed for our blood to clot properly when we do ourselves an injury and for our nerves to function properly. Children need a lot of calcium for developing bones and teeth as the skeleton increases in size up to the late teens. Even after the skeleton has stopped growing calcium continues to be added to our bones for several more years, enabling them to become denser and stronger. This can be seen on an X-ray. In our late thirties our bones start to become noticeably less dense and weaker, especially in women after the menopause, and in many elderly women the bones are so weak that even quite minor falls can result in fractures. The hip bone is especially vulnerable and a broken hip, known in medical circles as 'a fractured neck of the femur', is a serious hazard of growing old.

So where do we aim our trolley to ensure we get enough calcium to prevent our bones deteriorating? Would it were as simple as that! It would be nice if just increasing our consumption of calcium could keep our bones thick and strong as we get older, but unfortunately the situation is more complicated than this. Bone is not solid calcium as we might expect, but a living structure penetrated by muscle fibres and other living cells. To maintain the complex structure of our bones, regular exercise is essential as well as adequate supplies of vitamin D to ensure that the calcium can be efficiently absorbed from our intestines into our blood stream.

Milk and dairy products have long been hailed as the richest source of calcium, but plants obviously contain significant amounts of calcium too – otherwise how would elephants and rhinoceroses be able to build up and maintain their huge skeletons on a vegetarian diet. Milk, however, is one of the richest sources and the good news is that semi-skimmed and skimmed milk contain just as much calcium as full-fat milk, slightly more in fact. Another rich source is the bones of canned fish which have been softened by the canning process, and also hard water. Full-fat and semi-skimmed milk (but not skimmed) and fish also contain the vitamin D which is essential for the calcium to be absorbed properly from our intestines.

Ironing Out the Iron Problem

As we all know, a shortage of iron makes us anaemic. This is because iron is a component of haemoglobin, the substance that gives blood its red colour and that is packed into the red blood cells. Its job is to carry oxygen from the lungs around the body to where it is needed. Iron is also part of a similar substance in muscle that ensures that the muscles are kept supplied with oxygen. When we consume more iron than we need, we store it for a rainy day in our spleen, kidneys and liver.

Animals do the same, so you can guess what are especially rich sources – kidney and liver and liver products such as liver wurst and haggis, and blood products like black pudding. Good stuff haggis with all its iron, vitamin A and B12. No wonder the Scots are so good at throwing telegraph poles around at highland games – "caber tossing" they call it! Currants, sultanas and raisins are also iron-rich

There is no shortage of iron in everyday nosh either – fruit, vegetables and meat all supply respectable amounts. Manufacturers also add iron to breakfast cereals and certain other processed foods, ensuring that there is plenty of it around. The problem is that very little of the iron we eat actually succeeds in making its way through the wall of our intestines into our blood stream where it can be used. The type of iron in meat, fish and poultry is the most readily absorbed but even then we absorb less than a third of what we consume. With the iron present in plants, we are lucky if we absorb 10 per cent, and the amount varies considerably according to what else we happen to eat at the same time. Vitamin C, for instance, helps us to absorb iron, whereas the oxalic acid in rhubarb and spinach binds to it and holds it back. Remember when we were exploring the vegetable section I said that although spinach has about three times as much iron as most greens it is in a form which makes it difficult to absorb! Substances in unprocessed bran and the tannins in tea also make it more difficult for us to absorb iron. To boost your absorption of iron, follow some of your iron-rich meals with a glass of orange juice instead of a cup of tea, and include fruits and vegetables rich in vitamin C in as many meals as possible.

Anaemia due to a lack of iron can occur in young people who need it for growth as well as to replace daily losses. Women need more iron than men to replace that lost monthly in blood and also need more during pregnancy. Vegetarians tend to be more prone to iron deficiency than people who eat meat since they have to rely on the less readily absorbed type from plants. So if you are a young vegetarian about to pop a sprog make sure you are getting enough iron.

Take care in the use of iron supplements, however, as an excess of iron is of more immediate danger than a deficiency. The small proportion of its iron that is absorbed makes it difficult to obtain too much from food, but the highly concentrated source in iron tablets has been responsible for many cases of poisoning in young children. Iron supplements are best taken only on doctors' advice. Your family doctor can easily tell from the results of a simple blood test whether you need more iron or not, and it is pointless taking a supplement if you don't need it. If you do end up taking a supplement, it should be treated as a medicine and locked securely away.

Just a Trace

As remarked earlier, not only does our manufacturing industry depend on metals such as chromium, cobalt, copper, manganese, magnesium, molybdenum, selenium and zinc, but so do we. Their roles in the body are many and varied and the interactions between them so complex that there is considerable debate about whether mineral supplements are advisable or not. They may upset the balance and do more harm than good. Because we need them in such small amounts these metals are known as trace elements. Let us start by looking briefly at the best known of the trace elements, iodine, one of the few that is not, in fact, a metal.

Iodine

A lack of iodine causes goitre, a condition which manifests itself as an enlargement of the thyroid gland in the neck. The gland enlarges in an attempt to compensate for the lack of iodine, an essential component of one of its hormones. Women are more prone to goitre than men and it is most likely to appear at adolescence or during pregnancy.

Goitre was known in China as early as 3000BC and was effectively treated by feeding the affected persons seaweed, which we now know to be rich in iodine from sea water. In parts of the world where there is a tendency to goitre owing to a lack of iodine in the soil, such as Switzerland and parts of Canada, suppliers are required by law to add iodine to salt intended for human consumption. Despite this simple preventative measure, goitre still causes an enormous amount of suffering in certain parts of the world. Worse than the goitre itself, children born of mothers with malfunctioning thyroid glands due to severe iodine deficiency (or other causes) may have reduced stature and learning difficulties, the condition known as cretinism.

Goitre due to a lack of iodine is confined to parts of the world where most of the food comes from soils deficient in iodine, but this is not a problem in the UK or most parts of the USA. Cases of goitre here are not usually due to a simple lack of iodine but to a hormonal imbalance, so anyone noticing that they have a swollen thyroid should see their doctor before taking a supplement.

Zany Zinc

This trace element recently passed through one of those phases which most trace elements pass through at one time or another when it was being hailed as the cure for all our ills. Its place as a cure-all has now been taken by selenium, which we will talk about later.

Employed in industry as a coating for galvanised iron, as a component of flashlight batteries and, alloyed to copper, for making brass, in our bodies zinc has even more uses. A severe lack of zinc in the diet of children can results in stunted growth and loss of appetite. In adults it is needed to maintain the structure of the skin and for wound repair, and has been shown to be effective in the treatment of certain forms of acne in zinc deficient persons. A healthy balanced diet should provide all of the zinc we need, so if we experience such symptoms they are more likely to be due to some other cause than to a lack of zinc. Zinc is present in small amounts in virtually all foods, the richest sources being meat products and whole cereal grains. Zinc is lost when flour is refined, another good reason for eating wholemeal bread, which contains three times as much of the mineral as white bread.

Cobalt

Cobalt is an essential mineral right enough, but we need so little of it that it would be difficult to find anyone suffering from a severe deficiency. Interestingly, it is part of the structure of vitamin B12, and so long as we are getting enough B12 it would be difficult to get too little cobalt.

Magnificent Magnesium

Magnesium is in our bones, although only tiny amounts of it are needed for a healthy bone structure in comparison with calcium. We also need magnesium for transmitting impulses along our nerves, and for moving our muscles. Without it we would be in a bad way, but we are only likely to become deficient if we starve ourselves, suffer from severe alcoholism associated with self-neglect, or have inflammation of the pancreas, or prolonged diarrhoea and vomiting. It is found in almost all foods and is absorbed efficiently from our intestines into our blood.

Selenium

Selenium is now hailed as the wonder mineral because of the antioxidant properties it shares with the ACE vitamins. This metal has attracted a lot of attention in recent years since it joined the rank of the ever expanding army of antioxidants – the Free Radical Busters – credited with the ability to help defend us against cancer and heart disease. It is found in all seafood and meat and cereal grains. The amount in cereal grains, however, depends on the amount in the soil on which the cereal was grown. Canadian wheat from which a lot of British flour used to be made tended to contain far more selenium than the European wheat mostly used nowadays, so Britons may be getting less from this source than we used to. The selenium story is so complex that scientists have not yet been able to work out with any degree of confidence how much we should be consuming. The problem is that high doses of selenium are toxic. Animals grazing areas where the soil is rich in selenium can be poisoned by it, especially if they happen to consume the particular species of wild plants that have the uncanny knack of concentrating it, like Gray's vetch and woody aster.

Not Even a Trace

At the other extreme, a deficiency of certain trace elements can be a serious problem for sheep, cattle and other domestic animals that spend their lives consuming grass from one small area of land. If the soil is deficient in one or more of the trace elements symptoms of deficiency may arise, and mineral supplements have to be provided by the farmer. Cows grazing magnesium deficient grassland, for instance, become nervous, froth at the mouth and keel over, unless they are given an injection of magnesium salt by the vet. Human beings can experience mineral deficiencies when all of the food they consume is grown on deficient soil, but for the supermarket shopper consuming, as he or she inevitably will, a variety of foods grown in different parts of Britain and imported from around the world, devastating attacks of trace element deficiency are unlikely to arise. For this reason and because the amount of a trace element in a fruit or vegetable depends so strongly on the amount present in the soil in which it was grown, it would not be particularly helpful to provide a 'Where to aim your trolley' shopping list for trace elements.

Chapter 6

Eat More Wholemeal Bread and Breakfast Cereals

Who says, "Obtain at least half of your energy from starch"? The World Health Organisation says so. We have already done a lot of campaigning on behalf of starch-filled potatoes and root vegetables. We will now extend our support to other candidates. Getting our energy from starch also means eating lots of cereal products – wholemeal bread, rice, pasta and breakfast cereals such as Weetabix and Shredded Wheat. All are fine healthy foods that, like the original cereal grain, are packed with starch, protein and B vitamins. As a bonus, they contain hardly any fat.

The Bread of Life

Increase the amount of bread you eat by half – all of the extra bread being wholemeal, not white.

One of the best things to eat when you want an energy-rich snack is, wait for it, a slice of bread. The expression "the best thing *since* sliced bread" has always puzzled me. What was the best thing *before* sliced bread? Anyway, a loaf of wholemeal bread is packed full of starch for energy, has an abundance of body-building protein, numerous vitamins and minerals and hardly any saturated fat. What more could a body ask for? Now that the wheat flour used for making bread commercially is often supplemented with soya flour, the protein in bread is of an even higher quality than it used to be.

Drop some lettuce on your bread, some grated carrot, slices of apple, half-fat or cottage cheese. Even spread a thin layer of sticky honey, jam or marmalade which, although it might be bad for your teeth, will be much better for you than cake and biscuits. Or what about a banana sandwich; mash up the banana with a fork, add just a little sugar or some honey and spread it on the bread; delicious! Just look at all the different kinds of bread we have to choose from nowadays.

On Rosh Hashanah (the Jewish New Year) there is a service called Taslich (throwing) where adherents cast their sins away by throwing bread into the water. Some people ask what they are supposed to throw into the water. Here are one rabbi's suggestions.

- ✔ For ordinary sins – white bread
- ✔ For exotic sins – French or Italian bread
- ✔ For complex sins – multi-grain
- ✔ For sins of indecision - waffles
- ✔ For committing arson – toast
- ✔ For being ill-tempered – sourdough
- ✔ For silliness – nut bread
- ✔ For not giving full value – shortbread
- ✔ For excessive use of irony – rye bread
- ✔ For continual bad jokes – corn bread

Don't say it, if I were Jewish, I would need to stock up on the corn bread. Most of these breads are now available in a typical supermarket. Not so long ago, it was a choice between white sliced and white unsliced and perhaps Hovis brown. Now we are spoiled for choice with dozens of different breads adorning the shelves of a typical supermarket, almost all of them good, healthy, brown wholemeal. This is clear evidence that tastes can change for the better and that producers and retailers really are capable of responding to the challenge of providing a healthier diet.

It is not that white bread is bad for us. For the fussy few who don't like wholemeal bread it's infinitely better than eating no bread at all. White bread is just as rich a source of starch and protein as wholemeal bread. The reason that wholemeal is even better is that it is made from the whole cereal grain, whereas in making white flour, the husk, the outer part of the grain, is removed, as is the inner part, the wheatgerm. This matters because it is the husk and wheatgerm that contains most vitamin E, thiamine and other important vitamins. Wholemeal bread would contain more than twice as much thiamine as bread made from white bread were it not a legal requirement in the United Kingdom for white flour to be fortified with added thiamine.

It seems crazy to remove the vitamins only to have to add them back again! Some of the B vitamins including thiamine are replaced, as is calcium, but other vitamins and minerals present in the husk are not. Be a regular guy and eat wholemeal bread with 'nowt taken out', then you can be certain that you are getting all of the goodness that the cereal grain has to offer.

In addition to the vitamins, another advantage of husky wholemeal bread is that the husk provides fibre to facilitate the free passage of undigested wastes through the intestines. Not only does this mean less constipation, but fibre in the diet also helps protect against bowel cancer, possibly because, by increasing the speed at which waste passes through, it reduces the length of time that evil cancer-producing chemicals present in the waste are in contact with the bowel wall.

Many of these wholemeal breads are so tasty we can eat them by themselves without bothering with any spreads. I often partake of a slice of wholemeal bread when I feel like a snack instead of a biscuit or slice of cake. Spreading butter on bread is a great British tradition. Most of our European neighbours, however, take their bread neat, like a true Scotsman takes his whisky. Why then do we British insist on ruining a healthy, fat-free snack by slapping saturated fat all over it? Soft margarine, high in unsaturated fat is marginally better, but why bother when bread tastes so good neat.

Rice: the Staple Diet of Millions

"How would you like your rice?" asked the waiter.

"Thrown at me," the elderly spinster replied, wistfully.

As well as being traditionally thrown at weddings, rice is eaten by hundreds of millions of people throughout the world. For them it is their staple diet and they eat more rice than anything else, so it is obviously a very nutritious, high quality food which can provide the basis of a balanced diet if supplemented with reasonable amounts of vegetables and fruit and pulses. The problem is that in many of the rice eating countries there often isn't enough of these other foods to go round, a problem compounded by eating white rice instead of brown. When white polished rice with the seed coat removed became fashionable in South East Asia, people started to develop a condition called beriberi due to a deficiency of thiamine. As with wholemeal flour, it is far more sensible to eat whole grain, brown rice, rather than the impoverished white variety with many of the nutrients polished away.

Many of us in Britain enjoy the snap, crackle and pop of Rice Crispies and the occasional pudding, usually out of a tin. If it took our fancy, there are enough delicious recipes using rice to enable us to eat it regularly without becoming bored so that it provided us with a significant proportion of our energy.

Pasta

Pasta is another rich source of carbohydrate. Macaroni and spaghetti are full of starch, like the wheat grains from which they are derived, and well worth making part of our regular diet. The word 'pasta' means 'dough'. Most Italian-type pasta is made from semolina, part of the grain of durum wheat. During manufacture the semolina is mixed with warm water and kneaded into a dough, which is forced through perforated metal plates. The size and shape of the perforations in the plates, or dies, as they are called, determines the finished product. Forcing the dough through ring-shaped openings with central cores produces hollow, tubular forms of pasta like macaroni. Force the dough through smaller holes without cores and you get spaghetti; through letterbox-shaped holes and you get flat, ribbon-like pasta. After it is shaped, the dough is carefully dried to reduce the moisture content to about 12 per cent.

To make green pasta to serve up at an ecological convention, spinach is added to the dough; for red or pink pasta, tomatoes or beets are added; and for bright yellow pasta, eggs or turmeric. Extra wheatgerm, bran or gluten may also be added.

There are literally hundreds of different shapes and sizes of pasta, all with their own individual names. Italians have more names for pasta than Icelanders have for snowflakes. Amongst the most popular string type are spaghetti, which in Italian means 'little strings' and the appetisingly named vermicelli ('little worms').

Breakfast in a Box

Eat twice as much breakfast cereal. Not you or me necessarily but the population as a whole.

Like wholemeal bread, the best breakfast cereals consist of about 70 per cent starch, not surprisingly, as they share the same origin – the ubiquitous cereal grain. Sticking to the party line that we should be obtaining most of our energy from starch, the expert committees recommend that, as a nation, we should double our consumption of breakfast cereals.

Every supermarket has a library of cereal boxes with a bewildering array of titles filling several lengthy shelves. How do we choose from the dozens available? The simple answer would be to stick to the classics – Rice Crispies, Weetabix, Shredded Wheat, Wheat Puffs and Porridge Oats, virtually all starch with little or no added sugar.

Sugary Silliness

Not that I want to stifle a spirit of adventure, but many of the newer editions have so much sugar added that it would be just as realistic to look upon them as sugar with added cereal. You think I'm exaggerating, well there are dozens of breakfast cereals that, like Frosties (basically Corn Flakes with sugar), are specially designed to be appealing to children and contain a massive 40 per cent sugar. As for Sugar Puffs, almost exactly one half of these little monsters is sugar.

When choosing a breakfast cereal, read that label on the side of the packet to suss out how much sugar it contains. Go for the ones where the carbohydrate is nearly all starch, and persuade younger members of the family to do the same. Well, one can always live in hope! If you have any children in toe, try offering them a box of plain Puffed Wheat, the sugar-free equivalent of Sugar Puffs, and you may well be surprised at their reaction. I have seen kids brought up on sugared cereals find these sugar-free ones such a novelty that they eat them raw like crisps.

Salty Senselessness

To accompany the sugar, so many breakfast cereals also contain large amounts of salt applied willy-nilly by the manufacturers. As salt contributes to high blood pressure, older people and those with a tendency to high blood pressure are best to avoid it.

Now to draw up a shortlist of candidates for the job of filling the aspiring Mr Trim-Guy's cavernous stomach before he goes off to work – or the job centre – in the morning. We don't want sweet, salty types for the job in hand; we want tough guys with starch and fibre. Be like tough-guy John Major who, on being asked how he would start his first day as Prime Minister, replied, 'Eat three Shredded Wheat.'

In the first division are six cereals packed with starch and fibre but with little sugar or salt. They are the high fliers that have everything. Those cereals occupying the second and third divisions have both strengths and weaknesses. Those in the bottom division will only make their way up the league table if they rid themselves of some of their surplus sugar and salt.

Many of the sugary breakfast cereals also contain a cocktail of totally unnecessary colourings and flavourings and indigestible plastic toys! I am not getting at any partic-

Boxing Clever with Breakfast Cereals

Type of cereal	Sugars %	Sodium %	Fibre %
The best of both worlds: low in sugar AND low in salt			
Plain Puffed Wheat (Quaker)	0.3	0.0	6
Shredded Wheat (Nestle)	0.7	0.0	10
Ready Brek (Weetabix Ltd)	2	0.1	8
Whole Wheat Flakes (Safeways)	4	0.4	10
Weetabix (Weetabix Ltd)	5	0.3	10
Porridge Oats (Quaker)	1	0	7
Low in sugar: but high in blood pressure-raising salt			
Cornflakes (Kellogg's)	8	1.1	1.0
Rice Crispies (Kellogg's)	10	1.2	1
Special K (Kellogg's)	15	0.9	2
Plastered with tooth-rotting sugar: but low in salt			
Sugar Puffs (Quaker)	49	0	3
Weetos (Weetabix Ltd)	36	0.3	6
The worst of both worlds: high sugar AND high salt			
Coco Pops (Kellogg's)	38	0.9	2
Frosties (Kellog's)	40	0.9	1

ular manufacturer. As you can see from the table, each company produces both good, healthy breakfast cereals and nasty, sugary and salty ones. Don't be too disheartened though by the sugar and salt. Even the most sugary, saltiest breakfast cereals are arguably better than bacon and eggs as they are all virtually fat free and full of vitamins, some natural, others added by the manufacturer.

An acceptable compromise if you can't resist the sweeter, more colourful cereals is to start with a bowl of the basic, healthy cereal, say a couple of Weetabix, and sprinkle some of the others over it. That way, the overall sugar content remains lower and you will inflict on yourself a lower dose of colourings and flavourings than if you were to eat the alternative cereals neat.

Want to be adventurous, then there are some interesting recent additions to the cereal shelves. Say Hello to Cheerios in hoop-shaped bites made from a variety of different whole cereal grains – wheat, maize, oats and rice – all in the one packet. They have twice as much sugar as Cornflakes but less than half as much as Frosties, and a limited number of additives. They also taste good, so are probably worth a try.

The All-Day Breakfast

They are dubbed *breakfast* cereals, but a bowl of cereal with semi-skimmed or skimmed milk can be enjoyed at any time of day when we feel like a snack. Perhaps they are just a little bit messy to eat in the office and too much bother to have to keep prising out of the computer keyboard, but at home, no problem! Some cereals like Cheerios and Corn Pops can be nibbled raw without milk and added to the school lunch box as a healthier alternative to crisps. Although there is more sugar in them than reason dictates, they also contain a lot of starch and vitamins and are very low in fat and so are much better for young tums than crisps and snack bars.

Are You Getting Your Oats?

> *Land of the High Endeavour*
> *Land of the Lousy Weather*
> *Start off the day with piping Scott's porridge oats.*

So ran the words of one long-running television advertisement for a popular brand of porridge oats, or at least words to that effect – I've used a bit of poetic licence. As well as forming the basis of porridge, and being a component of the multi-cereal breakfast cereals, oats are also a component of muesli, another good healthy bowl of nosh we should be scooping up more of. Oats were the staple diet of the Scottish population before potatoes came along, and indeed were widely grown throughout the UK for human consumption.

What could be better than porridge oats with warm semi-skimmed milk to warm you up on a cold winter's morning. The English weather is just as bad, by the way. It's irritating though, is it not, how it seems impossible to combine the heating of milk with any other activity whatsoever. At whatever point you turn your back on it, it never fails to take advantage of your momentary lapse of attention to launch an escape bid over the sides of the pan, messing up the cooker and setting off the smoke detector.

Comparatively few oats are grown nowadays, which is a great pity because they are a good, nourishing food, containing lots of energy-yielding starch and body-building protein. Oats have twice as much fat as most cereals, but it is mostly the healthy unsaturated kind. Oats are also rich in insoluble fibre to keep your blood cholesterol levels down.

Keep them Bowels A'Moving

Although not quite the universal panacea for all our ills that our grannies might have had us believe, keeping the bowels moving is none the less highly desirable. And what do we need to do to keep our bowels moving, apart from bungee jumping? Yes, eat fibre, or roughage as it is sometimes called, and lots of it. Our digestive systems evolved to handle a diet high in fibre, that is, one containing lots of fruit and vegetables.

Fibre is indigestible and bulky, a waste of chewing effort you might think, but no. As it makes its way through the bowel it absorbs water and the increased bulk stimulates the nerves of the lower part of the intestine – the colon – creating the desire to pass stools more frequently, while their softness makes it easier to satisfy this desire.

Towards the end of the last century the fibre content of the average diet plummeted. White flours and sugar began to supply most of the carbohydrate content of the diet, supplanting the whole grain porridges and breads which people used to eat. To make matters worse, at the same time fruit and vegetable consumption fell too. As a result, constipation became rife. Few escaped the curse.

You will find fibre only in fruit and vegetables and grains, not in meat or meat products. So, for regular, readily ejected, satisfying stools eat plenty of fruit and vegetables, especially peas and beans, wholemeal bread and high fibre breakfast cereals.

Regular exercise will also help keep you regular on the bowel front, ask Mr Mot(ion Act)ivator.

Avoiding Gut Rot

As well as reducing the agony of constipation, and saving a lot of money in laxatives, consuming plenty of fibre may also help to prevent more serious disorders like irritable bowel syndrome, diverticulosis and diverticulitis. 'Divert – What! Let me explain. Diverticulosis is a condition in which tiny "balloons' bulge out from the walls of the large intestine; diverticulitis is when they then become inflamed. 'Itis' means inflammation, as in appendic*itis*. This results in abdominal pain that can be quite severe. The balloons arise because, in the absence of sufficient fibre, the contents of the gut are unnaturally small and hard. These hard pellets accumulate and stimulate the gut to contract but, contract as it will, it has great difficulty in pushing the pellets any further. Result: the gut builds up too much pressure, and although it doesn't actually explode, its walls blow out into these small protrusions. 'Diverticula' is just a fancy name for a small protrusion. Doctors, you will have noticed, are very fond of using erudite-sounding expressions to impress their patients. These diverticula or protrusions are very common and, like the appendix, only produce unpleasant symptoms if they become inflamed, producing diverticulitis.

Eating plenty of fibre so that you can perform your daily duty without straining also helps to reduce the risk of hiatus hernia and haemorrhoids. OK, this is good basic stuff. We can understand why plenty of fibre in the diet might help us avoid constipation, and diverticulosis and so on, what about all these other highfalutin claims that fibre helps to protect against heart disease and cancer. Aren't such claims a bit far fetched? Well, let's see if we can find a logical explanation for why the claims might be true. Let us forget cancer as a whole and concentrate on one form only, that of the colon.

Now let us assume that carcinoma of the colon is caused by carcinogens in the shit. How does fibre help? It absorbs water and increases the bulk of the stools, so diluting any dangerous chemicals that might produce cancer. It also speeds up the rate at which the waste passes through the colon and disappears down the toilet pan.

The combined result is that the cancer-producing chemicals are more likely to be eliminated from the body before they have time to cause any damage to the cells lining the inside of the colon. That's logical, but evidence that it helps protect against other kinds of cancer is more speculative and difficult to prove. High fibre diets are usually diets high in fruit and vegetables, which also contain vitamins and minerals which may themselves help to protect against cancer. So the observation that a population on a high fibre diet has a lower incidence of a certain kind of cancer is not proof that it is the fibre to thank; it could be the vitamins or other health giving substances in the fruit and vegetables. It might be a bit over-optimistic to assume that fibre supplements out of a tin would do much to protect against cancer in general.

And Artery Rot

What about the claim that fibre can reduce the risk of heart disease? How strong is the scientific evidence on which this claim is based? As we see in the 'Eggs Get a Beating' chapter, it is well established that people with high levels of cholesterol in their blood have a higher risk of heart disease, so we might expect anything that reduces blood cholesterol levels to reduce this risk. Fibre does just that; it lowers blood cholesterol. As it passes through the intestines soluble fibre binds to cholesterol, helping the body to eliminate it. This reduces cholesterol levels in the blood, which in turn reduces the deposition of cholesterol on the walls of the arteries that would eventually fur them up and constrict the blood supply. Sounds good, but does it work in practice, and reduce heart attacks? A lot of studies have shown that populations which consume lots of fibre suffer less heart disease than those who consume less, but again it's difficult to unravel to what extent this is due to the fibre and how much to the other goodies in the fruit and vegetables which people get their fibre from.

Eat Both Soluble and Insoluble – That's the Solution

Note I said 'soluble' fibre binds to cholesterol. So far we have been talking as though there is only one kind of fibre, but in reality there are two main types, soluble, which surprise, surprise, dissolves in water, and insoluble, which doesn't. Most fruits and vegetables contain both kinds, but in different proportions. Beans and peas, oats, barley and some fruits, especially apples and oranges are high in the soluble variety that binds cholesterol. So are potatoes. Just the thing for reducing your risk of heart disease. If you are more concerned about cancer of the colon, foods containing high levels of insoluble fibre to whiz your stools along, are wheat bran, cereals, seeds and the skins of many fruits and vegetables.

Eat a good variety of fruit and vegetables and wholewheat bread and breakfast cereals and you'll get plenty of both kinds of fibre without thinking about it. Books have been written on how to achieve a high fibre diet, but it's really very simple. Here is our five-point high fibre plan:

✔ Start the day with a whole grain breakfast cereal like All-Bran, Shredded Wheat or Weetabix. Alternatively, what about some muesli with oats and nuts and fruity bits, all of which are high in fibre, or, from the land of the caber-tossing Scots, why not tuck into some porridge.

✔ Eat raw vegetables whenever possible. Over cooking can reduce the fibre by breaking it down into smaller substances. If cooking, go gently. We know cooks are a violent lot; they beat their eggs, whip their cream, and batter their fish, but vegetables should always be treated gently.

✔ Avoid peeling fruit and vegetables: the skins contain a lot of fibre. But wash them first in warm water to remove dirt and bacteria, pesticides, herbicides, fungicides, and any other -icides, that might be there.

✔ Eat plenty of wholemeal bread, cereals and pasta.

✔ Get into the bean habit. There are lots of different kinds to choose from. Add them to soups, stews and salads. A standard can of baked beans (410g) contains over 15g fibre, a third soluble, the rest insoluble. Use frozen peas and beans as well. Take them out of the freezer, pop them into boiling water, leave for a few minutes, pour on to a plate and scoff.

✔ Always have fresh fruit and vegetables handy for a snack. Include berries and currants, which have lots of fibre.

Sorry, that's six points.

Having decided to take the plunge and increase the amount of fibre in your diet, be warned. Do so gradually over a period of weeks or months to give your digestive system time to adapt, otherwise you may end up with abdominal discomfort and even diarrhoea. You might even think fibre doesn't agree with you, and give up. And that would never do.

Disgusting Digestion

Our digestive system operates like a complex chemical works that enables our bodies to make use of the food we eat. Digestion starts in the mouth, where the action of chewing breaks down food into smaller pieces and the enzymes in saliva break down starch into sugar. That is why starchy foods like bread begin to taste sweet if we chew them for a long time.

On the arrival of food in the stomach, digestion is begun in earnest. After being churned up with acid and more enzymes which break down the protein into amino acids, the food is passed out of the stomach into the small bowel. Although called the 'small' bowel, at an incredible six metres long, over three times the length of an average person, it is anything but small. How surgeons who perform operations on the small bowel ever manage to fit it all back in again beats me! In the small bowel the food is flooded with yet more enzymes which break it down into simple sugars and fats and amino acids, the building blocks of protein, which are absorbed through its walls into the blood stream.

Undigested waste wends its way along to the colon, in whose dark and eerie chamber it is attacked by colonies of native bacteria, and excess water and minerals are absorbed back into the body. The remaining waste is compacted and passed along to the departure lounge, the rectum, and, when we have a few quiet moments to ourselves, ejected via the anus, along with masses of the bacteria. The journey from mouth to anus takes between a day and a half and three days, longer if you are constipated. So, if you ever accidentally swallow anything valuable, be patient! The resultant faeces, poo, shit, call it what you will, then commences an equally long and tortuous journey to the sea, but that is beyond the scope of this book.

Chapter 7

Let's Take a Butcher's at Meat

The government's advice to the Fat Teeth of Britain: reduce by half the amount of processed meat and sausages you eat. Mr Fat-Tooth typically devours a lot of meat. So what, isn't meat good for a growing lad, providing the protein to build up big, strong, healthy muscles, and the iron for rich, red blood? True, meat is an excellent source of first-class protein – but remember, gorillas do quite well without it -. You may wonder how we can possibly eat too much of it, and resent the suggestion that it might be bad for us. After all, human beings have been devouring the animals with whom they share the planet for millions of years, so doesn't that mean that meat is a natural food which must be good for us?

Pigs, Sheep and Cattle: The Fearsome Fat Three

The key to this apparent contradiction lies in the fact that the meat we eat today is so very different from the meat our ancestors ate. Our meat comes mainly from three species – sheep, cattle and pigs – not from the wild game that the hunter-gatherers of old consumed. But why should this make a difference? The reason is that present-day sheep, cattle and pigs are fat, incredibly fat, compared to their lean wild relatives, just like Mr and Mrs Fat-Tooth. Over a quarter (25 per cent) of the meat we obtain from these domesticated animals is fat, in sharp contrast to the wild game, the rabbits, deer, wild goats and other wild animals, that our ancestors used to eat, which all contained less than 5 per cent. It so happens that virtually all wild animals that live and feed on land contain less than 5 per cent fat. Ironically, out of the several thousand species of mammals in the world, the three that we eat most of are the worst for us, and the most fattening.

With a pound of beef or pork containing five times as much fat as a pound of rabbit or venison, to say that people have always eaten meat so it can't be bad for us is ridiculous. The meat that people used to eat until a few generations ago was so much healthier than the fat lamb, beef and pork that is mostly eaten today that there is no comparison.

Venison is, of course, still around with us today, and with deer farms springing up around the country is becoming more readily available. Deer are farmed in much the same way as cattle, with the animals spending most of their time grazing out of doors, with the difference that farmed deer are virtually indistinguishable from their wild relatives. They have not been exposed to generations of selective breeding to expand their fat content. The ecological problem posed by overstocking of the Highlands – the deer eat the young seedlings and prevent the regeneration of natural woodland – has meant that wild venison is now available not only in specialist butchers, but from some supermarkets.

On seeing venison on sale at the local supermarket, Jane bought some to try because her children had never tasted it. She cooked it and, to make a game of it, asked her husband, Mike, to make the children guess what it was. Mike came up with all sorts of different hints but the children failed to get the answer. Finally, he had a brainwave, "It's what your Mom sometimes calls me," he said. On hearing this, daughter Kirsty turns to her brother in alarm and shouts, "Spit it out quick, Andrew, it's arsehole."

Why are the sheep, cattle and pigs of the twenty-first century so fat? I can offer at least two explanations for this. Years of selective breeding is one. In order to produce meat that's as tender as possible, animal breeders have repeatedly bred from fatter animals. In successive generations the beasts have progressively become fatter and fatter. Also, before vegetable oils became so readily available in Britain, there was a big demand for fat in the form of lard for cooking, and remember that in the olden days, before we all had electric lighting, fat was highly prized for making candles.

So what's the problem? Fat was bred into them, so couldn't it just be bred out of them again? Yes, it could be if there was sufficient financial incentive, like consumers refusing to spend their money on fat cuts of meat. A number of agricultural research establishments have been applying their talents towards breeding leaner pigs with some success, but they still have an extremely long way to go to get them back down to the wild boar level.

Another reason why domestic animals are so fat is intensive feeding and lack of exercise. Fed so intensively and needing to take so little exercise to obtain their food and to keep warm, they naturally become fatter, just like Mr and Mrs Fat-Tooth and their kids. Over-eating, and under-exercising is the universal recipe for obesity, in pigs as in people.

Most pigs are reared intensively in specially built pig houses. A high temperature is maintained in these houses to ensure that most of the food being provided automatically from hoppers goes into increasing weight rather than keeping warm. Under this system, neither the sows nor the growing pigs ever go outside. Pigs being fattened for the butcher are usually slaughtered at six months of age if they are being sold for bacon; those going for pork are dispatched some weeks earlier.

The outdoor system of pig production, under which the pigs are kept outside with small corrugated iron huts known as arks for shelter, is, however, gaining in popularity. They are allowed to forage for some of their own food and there are generally less health problems than with intensively reared pigs. The disadvantage of this system – for the farmer rather than the pigs – is that the pigs do not reach killing weight so quickly as they do in a warm house.

Bacon pigs do not, however, have such a healthy lifestyle. Free-range bacon is hard to come by.

Cattle, from Mountain Side to Veal Crate

As with pigs, the range of conditions under which cattle are kept varies enormously, from those which spend most of their days out in the open fields to the veal calves which spend the whole of their lives indoors in heated houses. Most of the veal eaten in Britain comes from Holland where the crate system still operates. Food is provided as a soup in water and the temperature kept high so that the calves will keep eating in an effort to obtain the water they need to quench their thirst. Their movements are constrained so that as little as possible of their food is 'wasted' to provide energy for movement, instead of being used to put on weight. Under such an intensive system they are ready for slaughter at between 13 and 20 weeks of age. Although the most intensive crate system is banned in Britain, British dairy calves are still exported to Europe, reared in the very system that has been banned here, and then re-imported as veal, a practice which has aroused tremendous opposition from people concerned about animal welfare.

Some cattle fare better, spending most of their days grazing the pastures and just coming indoors for supplementary feeds. The farmer pages them from the comfort of the barn to let them know when lunch is served. You think I'm joking don't you? Cows can be trained to associate the bleep of a pager with food so that when the farmer dials their number, those with the pagers around their necks come trotting in and the rest follow. Not yet universal practice, but it has been done.

Mad Cow Disease

Mad cow disease, or Bovine Spongeform Encephalopathy (BSE) as the scientists prefer to call it, first came to light in November 1986 when cattle starting going down with a strange neurological disease. In the following ten years around 150,000 cases were confirmed in the UK. Epidemiological studies suggested that the source of the disease was cattle feed prepared from the carcasses of dead cattle and sheep. Which of the two species it arose from has never been established.

More correctly, therefore, mad cow disease should be referred to as mad farmer's disease. A five-year-old child knows not to feed its pet hamster with meat. Hamsters are vegetarians and so are cattle, so what possessed farmers to feed their cattle and sheep on dead cattle and sheep?

BSE is transmitted from animal to animal but the agent is not a bacterium and it is not a virus. It is harder to kill than either of these, being resistant to pasteurisation, sterilisation, freezing and drying and to normal cooking temperatures.

Cases of BSE were not confined to the UK. By October 1996 it had been reported in 10 countries around the world. Embarrassingly, all of these cases were blamed either on cattle imported from the UK or on imported cattle feed. It was all our fault. In 1988, the UK government banned farmers from feeding live cattle and sheep with dead cattle and sheep. The following year it banned the use of brain and spinal cord, as well as tonsil, thymus, spleen and intestine of cattle from foods intended for human consumption.

BSE is not the only brain disease that can be transmitted between animals. Scrapie, a common disease of sheep, is another. Mink suffer from a similar neurological disease, and in North America, so do elk and mule deer, and recently, a similar disease has been identified in pet cats in the UK.

Human beings also fall victim to diseases that result in sponge-like changes to the brain visible under a microscope. Kuru is one of them. As the World Health Organisation put it in a recent report, kuru is "transmitted by human ritual handling of bodies and brains of the dead," or to put it more bluntly, by eating the brains of dead relatives and friends. As most mourners in the UK prefer a ham sandwich and a pint of beer, we cannot be blamed for that one. The second condition Creutzfeldt-Jakob Disease (CJD for short) is, however, present nearer home. Ironically, although most cases occur sporadically with no obvious cause, a group of people became affected in the UK as a result of being injected, as part of their medical treatment, with growth hormone extracted from the brains of dead human beings.

The discovery of a new form of CJD, labelled V-CJD, in ten patients in the UK in 1996 created quite a stir, and engendered fears of an epidemic to rival the Black Death of the Middle Ages. While scientists could find no definite link between BSE and the new form of CJD, circumstantial evidence suggested that exposure to BSE was the most likely cause. Around the same time, scientists showed that the BSE agent extracted from the brains of cattle could cause a similar disease when injected into experimental animals; so it could be transmitted to other species. Fortunately, as we enter the new millennium the dreaded epidemic has not yet materialised.

Now that feeding live cattle and sheep with dead cattle and sheep has been banned, and the brain and other parts of the cattle likely to contain the agent are no longer on sale, exposure to BSE has been greatly reduced. Just how safe it is to eat beef nowadays no one really knows.

Lambs – Soon Ready for the Chop

The happy, carefree, gambolling lambs seen chasing each other over the hillside appear to fare better, apart from the fact that they are on death row, but with no chance of a last minute reprieve. They will be allowed to live only for about five months, by which time they will weigh about 37 kilograms and be ready for the chop. You don't often find mutton – defined as meat from sheep over one year old – in the supermarkets nowadays. Shoppers tend to prefer the smaller, more tender cuts and farmers prefer not to keep stock over winter if it can be avoided. Sheep kept for their wool fare somewhat better in the longevity stakes. Puzzling isn't it, why sheep don't shrink after long hours on a rainy hillside.

Oozing Fat

Next time you pass by the meat counter in your local supermarket, note what I mean about saturated fat. You will see it oozing from the pork, the beef, the sausages, the meat pies, the mince, the corned beef, possibly even the butcher behind the counter if he overindulges in his own product. Twenty five per cent is the *average* amount of fat in cattle, pig and sheep meat. So-called "lean" cuts are at one end of the range with around 15 per cent fat, and at the other is fatty bacon with a massive 40 per cent fat. The Fat-Tooths will go for the fat end of the spectrum, aspiring Mr and Mrs Trim-Guys for the lean cuts.

The Vitamin-Rich Innards

Liver is worth eating in moderation for its vitamin A, vitamin B12 and iron, in all of which it is exceptionally rich. Mince the heart, lungs and liver of a sheep or deer together and mix with suet, oatmeal, onions, salt and pepper, then boil in a skin like that of a sausage and what do you have? I'll give you a clue:

> *Fair fa' your honest, sonsie face,*
> *Great chieftain o the puddin'-race!*
> *Aboon them a' ye tak your place,*
> *Painch, tripe, or thairm:*
> *Weel are ye wordy of a grace*
> *As lang's my arm.*

Yes, you've got it. It's the haggis. The poem above is Robert Burns' 'Address to the Haggis', recited with great gusto at every Burns' supper. It used to be enjoyed all over Britain, but is now considered a Scottish delicacy. Haggis is an excellent source of iron, vitamin A and vitamin B12 from the heart and liver. Pity it's high in fat and cholesterol, but a little occasionally will do us no harm.

Low-Flying, Low-Fat Chickens

One item on the meat counter that does not ooze fat is chicken. Chicken meat (excluding the skin) contains comparatively little fat, 5 per cent overall. Yes, that's about the same as wild game such as deer and rabbits. With meat from sheep, cattle and pigs containing around five times as much, it is obvious why it's healthier to eat poultry. Why choose red meat when there is a low-fat chicken right beside it at a lower price per pound! An occasional Sunday joint won't do us any harm, but if we eat meat regularly most of it should be poultry. Poultry liver, although often discarded, is just as valuable a source of vitamins and iron as sheep or ox liver with the added advantage that it comes free.

Millions now worship at the altar of the Sunday roast chicken; about half a billion chickens are sold each year in Britain. The success of the chicken is largely due to the fact that it lends itself well to mass processing techniques. The live chicken enters the plant and is carried along suspended from a belt past a slaughterer who cuts its throat. It is dipped into boiling water to loosen its feathers, then plucked by special rollers. It is then cut open, inspected and cleaned, and passed through a flame to burn off the pin feathers and hairs. It is then refrigerated and sent to market. The development of mass production plants means that chickens are now available to the consumer at a fraction of what in real terms they used to cost. If that is success, I would rather be a failure.

Free-range poultry in Britain are a little more expensive than battery-bred, but not a lot extra really for a finer taste, even lower fat and a clearer conscience. The breeds are specially selected for their slower growth rates and meat quality. The best will be fed on a minimum of 75 per cent cereal to enhance their natural flavour and reared in shaded open-air fields and woodlands for around three months. This is twice the life span of battery-bred birds, which are normally slaughtered at six weeks. Such birds should have firmer flesh, leaner skin and superior flavour. In France, traditional free-range guineafowl, duck, goose, quail and turkey are also readily available.

The Turkey: The National Bird of America – Nearly

The poultry doesn't always have to be chicken. Pheasants and turkeys, sporting even less fat than chickens, are no longer just a Christmas sacrifice but are now available all the year round, and can be purchased whenever we feel like a change of victim. Most supermarket chains now stock free-range turkeys, although not necessarily in every store.

Turkeys, by the way, did not originate in Turkey, but are a North American bird. The turkey nearly became the national bird of America; Benjamin Franklin advocated the adoption of the turkey rather than the eagle, which he said was 'a bird of bad moral fibre'.

High-Flying, High-Fat Quackers and Gabblers

Don't get swept away with the idea that all poultry are low in fat. Avoid ducks and geese, except as a special treat. These quackers and gabblers have on board a lot more fat than other domestic poultry. It helps to keep them warm and afloat. In some birds, the amount of fat they carry varies with the season. Migratory birds build up large reserves of fat to fuel their long-distance flights; fat on take off, by the time they reach their destination they are pretty lean.

Most supermarket ducks and geese are not shot on the wing but factory farmed, with the birds kept, although not in cages, under very restricted conditions. A small number of supermarkets sell free-range ducks and geese in selected stores, at least at Christmas.

Burying Your Head in the Sand

Ostriches never in reality do that, so I am told. Anyway, ostrich farms are now springing up all over the UK. You'll need a forklift truck to get it home from the supermarket and have to invest in a bigger oven to cook it. You'll also need to develop a large circle of friends to help you get it all eaten up, but most people find the meat an interesting change from normal and it is low in fat.

A Calorie-Saving Tip

Aspiring Mr and Mrs Trim-Guy, here's another calorie-saving tip. When eating chicken or turkey, to keep your fat consumption really low, don't eat the skin. Why not? Because the skin contains more than its fair share of the fat. Remove the skin before cooking if you can. If not, remove it before eating the rest of the chicken. The white meat contains very little fat and what there is, is mostly unsaturated, the good kind.

Ducks and geese, as we have already seen, are higher in fat than most poultry and a less desirable buy from a nutritional point of view. At the other end of the spectrum, pheasants, turkeys and ostriches are even leaner than chickens.

Cut-Throat Competition

During the last few decades the trend has been in the right direction from a nutritional viewpoint with the poultry producers stealing a larger and larger share of the market from the meat producers. Today's carnivorous Briton buys only half as much lamb, beef and veal as he did twenty years ago, while consuming twice as many poultry. The number of pigs biting the dust has, however, remained much the same.

Samosa aux Larves de Tenebrions

What a delightful-sounding exotic dish! Indeed it is, mealworms in deep fried pastry. Here's another for afters: criquet a la mexicaine. You can imagine the active ingredient of this, a cricket or some other member of the locust family.

Should we be eating more insects. Man has always eaten insects, if not by choice, then at least as part of the vegetation. When I was at school, lettuces always entered the home complete with a colony of caterpillars. It was usually possible to wash off most of these under the tap but there were always tiny spiders and other creatures that resisted the deluge. Cabbages and cauliflowers were always soaked in salt to winkle out slugs. Remember it; these were the good old days. Despite the preparation, insects and other wee beasties always got consumed.

Now that saturation bombing of horticultural plots with insecticides is the norm, are we missing out on something good; did insects provide an essential ingredient of our diet? Your guess is as good as mine.

Some people still eat insects, of course. You can pick up barbecued locusts from street traders in Bangkok, while silk workers in China often snack on the worms from which they derive the silk. Indeed, honey is not entirely insect free and the red dye, cochineal, still to be found in some alcoholic drinks, biscuits, cakes and icing is an extract of insects.

Most of us have seen those intrepid travellers to Australia on our TV sets tucking into the odd Wichery grub. It seems an obligatory part of any visit to the Australian outback. Seeing someone eat a live grub does nothing to encourage the incorporation of insects into our diet; after all, we don't eat live chickens do we? They are killed and cooked first. Once the same fate befalls insects they are no more nauseating to eat than prawns and shellfish.

For the insect gourmet, there is an Insectarium in Montreal, Canada, where they have festivals when you can sample various delightful dishes like those mentioned above that include insects amongst their ingredients. "Once past the exoskeleton and the fibrous hind legs, the locust is surprisingly creamy and firm, reminiscent of a slightly runny omelette that's been spiked with hot sauce." So ran Taras Grescoe's description of *cricket a la mexicaine,* one of the Montreal treats, writing in British Airways' *Highlife* magazine.

An Ethical Dilemma

As the French experience clearly shows that the rearing of poultry under humane conditions to supply the bulk market is a commercial proposition, is there really any good reason why all of the poultry sold in Britain should not be free-range? This would make the consumption of poultry rather than beef, pork and lamb a clear winner from the animal welfare as well as from the nutritional viewpoint.

The only satisfactory answer at present to the animal welfare question is to become a vegetarian. Failing that, from the nutritional point of view, as we approach the meat counter we should think poultry. If it proves impossible to resist the joint of beef, mutton or pork, go for the leanest cuts. The meat section of the Seek and Reduce Calorie and Fat Counter is there to help you choose. Avoid the cuts with lots of visible fat and trim off any you can see when you get home. Visible fat is mostly saturated fat so it is well worth removing. Not that any cut of the Fearsome Fat Three is really lean compared with the athletic leanness of wild game or poultry. Why not save yourself some money by buying a smaller joint, then nip back to the vegetable section for some extra spuds and greens to make up the difference.

Don't be a Kamikaze Pillock

It won't do any harm to tuck into a Sunday joint with plenty of veg., or a traditional cooked breakfast once in a while. But only kamikaze eaters should have daily bacon and eggs for breakfast – fat and cholesterol without the fresh vegetables -and the advice must be to avoid as completely as possible meals based on processed red meat like sausages, burgers, cans of luncheon meat and meat pies, which all contain masses of saturated fat. Incidentally, something that's always puzzled me: why did kamikaze pilots wear helmets?

Warming up with a hot dog at the funfair on a cold winter's night won't do us any harm, but if we want to keep our intake of saturated fat down, we certainly don't want to make a regular habit of processed meat.

If you want to find out more about the welfare of the animals sold for food, I can heartily recommend Audrey Eyton's *The Kind Food Guide*, published by Penguin in 1991.

Chapter 8

Fat – Friend or Foe?

"Saturated fats, polyunsaturated fats, essential fatty acids;" it can all become a bit bewildering to say the least. So, let us see if we can unravel the difference between the potentially harmful saturated fats in red meat and the various kinds of unsaturated fats that in sensible amounts are good for us. It's not really difficult. Once you get the idea, it's as simple as an income tax return.

The Sad Sat. Fats – The Bad Guys

Yes, Mr and Mrs Fat-Tooth, saturated fats will not only make you fat but they will go for the jugular, and every other blood vessel in the body for that matter. They will conspire with cholesterol to form plaques which narrow the arteries and make it more likely that the flow of blood will one day abruptly cease.

The main source of saturated fat, as you know by now, is the Fearsome Fat Three – pigs, cattle and sheep. Saturated fat is found in their meat, both joints and processed meat like sausages and burgers. It is found in their milk and in full-fat dairy products.

Keep within the Sat. Fat Feed Limit!

Take it from me, Mr and Mrs Fat-Tooth, fats of the saturated variety are bad for you. But don't just take my word for it. Convincing evidence has been gathered by scientists around the world that populations who eat large amounts of saturated fat develop more heart disease than those whose diet is low in saturated fat. The World Health Organisation recommends that we should obtain no more than one tenth (10 per cent) of our energy from saturated fat. So, how do we work that out? It's easy, even for a mathematical moron like myself.

Supposing you use 1,800 kcal of energy a day, about the average for a female, drive to work, keyboard-stomper, and no more than 180 kcal should be derived from saturated fat. As one gram of fat gives us 9 kcal, it is easy to calculate the maximum amount of saturated fat we are allowed to eat. Just divide 180 by 9. That gives us 20 grams. So, if we are averagely active adults let us set 20 grams as our daily limit of saturated fat.

Now I know that 1,800 kcal is about the average female requirement and that men, at least active ones, tend to use more energy, about 2,500 kcal per day. But as the World Health Organisation's 10 per cent is a maximum, let's err on the side of caution and set 20 grams as the daily saturated fat limit for the aspiring Mr Trim-Guy too.

Younger children and people who are less active and, therefore, need less energy should eat less saturated fat, but the converse does not apply. Oh no, a high level of activity does not supply the excuse for eating more fat. The active must satisfy their additional energy needs by eating more starch.

Twenty is a good, easy number to remember as it's the same as the new long-awaited speed limit being introduced in certain built up areas. But remember, Mr

and Mrs Fat-Tooth, that the saturated fat limit, like the speed limit, is an absolute maximum. Confining ourselves to 10g saturated fat today does not allow us to eat 30g tomorrow, any more than driving at 10mph today would allow us to exceed the speed limit tomorrow. An increased risk of obesity now and of heart disease in later life are the penalties for exceeding the *feed* limit. To be on the safe side we should keep well below the limit – whether it's miles per hour or grams of saturated fat per day.

Now for a few yardsticks to help us get a feel for what 20 grams of saturated fat looks like.

✔ A litre (just over two pints) of full-fat milk contains about 24g of saturated fat (40g total fat).

✔ Full-fat cheese contains approximately 22g of saturated fat in every 100g (34g total fat).

✔ Meat from a pig, sheep or cow contains on the average about 12g saturated fat in every 100g (25g total fat).

✔ Poultry, in contrast, (excluding the skin) contains only about 2g of saturated fat in every 100g (5g total fat).

If you are still used to thinking in terms of pounds and ounces, 100 grams is about 3.5 ounces.

Although twenty grams of saturated fat is a fairly generous limit, millions of people in Britain today consume far more. We derive, on the average, 16 per cent of our energy from saturated fat, way above the maximum of 10 per cent recommended by the World Health Organisation. Northern England and the West of Scotland are top of the saturated fat intake league.

Scientists who conduct research on the effect of diet on heart disease agree that the damage can begin when we are young, so the earlier we start on a healthy diet the better. On the other hand, it is never too late to mend our ways. At whatever age, Mr and Mrs Fat-Tooth see the light, their heart and circulatory systems will start to benefit. If you still drink full-fat milk, the simplest first step towards a low-fat diet is to switch to semi-skimmed milk. Next, cut down on the bacon and eggs, butter, cream, processed meats, biscuits and cake. If you did not make a New Millennium Resolution to cut down on the saturated fat, do it now.

The Terrible Trans-Fatty Acids in Horrible Hydrogenated Vegetable Oil

Some more bad guys! You may have seen hydrogenated vegetable oil printed on packets of margarine and on the labels of a wide variety of processed food and wondered what it meant. I'll tell you. Hydrogenated vegetable oil is polyunsaturated vegetable oil which the manufacturers have treated with hydrogen – hydrogenated – to convert some of the polyunsaturated fat into a kind of saturated fat called trans-fatty acids. These trans-fatty acids are at least as bad for us as natural saturated fat.

Why ever would anyone want to convert healthy polyunsaturated fat into saturated? The answer is to make the vegetable oil solid at room temperature. Vegetable oil is liquid because it contains mainly polyunsaturated fat, whereas butter is solid because it is largely saturated fat. Margarine is in between. Margarine is made from vegetable oils by hydrogenating them to convert some of the unsaturated fats into saturated fat so that the margarine is solid at room temperature. Although margarine still has much of the unsaturated fat of the vegetable oil, the saturated ones created chemically by the manufacturers are at least as bad for us as those in butter.

The take-home message is that margarine is preferable to butter, but we still need to go easy on it. Always read that label and choose those brands with the smallest amount of trans-fatty acids. Unfortunately, many brands still fail to provide this vital information. Express your disapproval by not buying them.

What level of trans-fatty acids should we be aiming for? Well, at least one light margarine has got its trans-fatty acids down to 0.4g in every 100g, so there is no need to buy margarine which contains more than that. Margarine is naturally a good source of Vitamin E because the oils it is made from are rich in the vitamin. It is also supplemented with vitamins A and D by the manufacturers to make sure that we do not miss out on these vitamins by spreading margarine instead of butter.

Aspiring Mr and Mrs Trim-Guy should remember that despite its healthier fat profile, low trans standard margarine is as calorie laden as butter, about 740 kcal per hundred grams. However, half-fat (and therefore half calorie) and even a few one-third fat varieties are available. To reduce the fat content of margarine, manufacturers need to add water, so low-fat varieties are best for spreading on your bread rather than for cooking. In one respect the low-fat spreads are not such good value, as much of what you are buying is water. But on the other hand, if you are committed to limiting your fat intake, and the water allows you to do just that while still providing the longed for margarine taste, so much the better.

Don't be a Fat-Free Freak

Aim to reduce the amount of sad saturated and terrible trans fats that you eat, but don't aim for a fat-free diet. Too much saturated fat is bad for our arteries, but fat of the unsaturated variety should be seen as an essential part of a normal healthy diet. Fat is an essential component of our cell membranes and is needed to absorb fat soluble vitamins A and D, and an array of other substances which may well be beneficial (like the antioxidant lycopene, found in tomatoes) from the intestines through into the blood stream.

Perfectly Presentable Polys

Polyunsaturated fat is found in just about every natural food, plant as well as animal, and in normal amounts is part of a healthy diet. The most concentrated sources of polyunsaturated fat are cooking oils and margarine. Anyone who eats lots of margarine or fried food could easily consume far more polyunsaturated fat than would be usual on a natural diet. As anything in excess may be harmful in the long term, it is a wise precaution not to overdo the cooking oil or margarine.

Marvellous Mediterranean Monos

In France, Spain, Italy and Greece and other Mediterranean countries where virtually the whole population munch their way through lots of fresh fruit and vegetables and where most of the fat they eat is unsaturated, there is a very low incidence of heart disease. This is even the case in places like the Greek island of Crete where the diet is very high in total fat.

Mediterranean folk tend to consume a lot of monounsaturated fats. Like polyunsaturated, monounsaturated fat is found in most plant and animal foods. A particularly rich source is olive oil, large amounts of which are consumed in the Mediterranean countries, the very places that happen to have the lowest incidence of heart disease. It would be hasty at this stage to jump in with claims that monounsaturated fat protects against heart disease, but we may safely assume that it is less damaging to the heart and circulatory system than saturated fat. So far as is known, monounsaturated fat is not harmful to health in any other way, but everything in moderation!

Rapeseed oil is as rich in monounsaturated fat as olive oil and both these oils are the basis of several brands of high mono margarines that have recently come onto the market.

Mono Margarines

The current trend is for the manufacturers to enhance the healthy image of their margarines by reducing the levels of polyunsaturates in favour of monounsaturated, as these are now thought to be healthier than polyunsaturated. The two commonly used vegetable oils with the highest proportion of monounsaturated are olive oil and rapeseed oil. While olives are very much a Mediterranean crop, we are all familiar with the mass of bright yellow flowers produced by our own rape crop that adorn the fields in spring, generating clouds of pollen that gets up some people's noses.

Margarine made from olive oil is generally recognisable by its name, for example, Tesco's 'Olive Gold' and Heinz 'Weight Watchers Olivite'. Manufacturers who use rapeseed oil clearly have an identity crisis. St Ivel Rape sounds like a horror headline in a West Country newspaper so, not surprisingly, manufacturers St Ivel opted to call their rapeseed oil margarine simply MONO.

Essential Fatty Acids: Good for the Heart

But hold on, we haven't finished yet. There is a fourth group of fats known as *essential* fatty acids that have attracted a lot of attention in recent years. These are a kind of unsaturated fat. They are called *essential* fatty acids because, as we are not able to make them within our own bodies, it is essential to have them in the diet.

The Omega-3 essential fatty acids are especially interesting in that they reduce the tendency of the blood to clot and may, therefore, help to protect against heart attacks. Small amounts are found in most types of food, but oily fish are especially rich in the Omega-3 essential fatty acids. This is why people who have had a heart attack are advised by their doctors to eat lots of oily fish to reduce their risk of a recurrence.

Cooking Oils

When Granny was a lass, just about everyone in Britain used lard or, if they were well off, butter for cooking, so every time they cooked or baked anything they saturated it with saturated fat. Fortunately, today there is an amazing variety of vegetable oils to choose from. For general cooking purposes we have sunflower oil, corn oil, ground-nut oil, grapeseed oil and olive oil, and from Britain's own oilfields, rapeseed oil. Numerous others like walnut oil, sesame oil, and safflower oil are used more sparingly to impart special flavours.

Vegetable cooking oils triumph over butter and lard in that although they consist entirely of fat, most of it is healthy unsaturated. As well as being better for the heart and circulatory system, unsaturated fatty acids are also said to be good for the joints. Apparently they stop them squeaking. The only common exceptions to the rule are coconut oil, in which 90 per cent of the fat is saturated, followed by palm oil, but these can easily be avoided. All cooking oils have virtually the same total amount of fat and the same number of calories, they differ only in the relative proportions of the different kinds of fat.

In olive oil, grapeseed and rapeseed oil two thirds of the fat is monounsaturated, while in most of the other vegetable oils, two thirds of it is polyunsaturated. People living on a Mediterranean-type diet consuming a fair amount of olive oil tend to have lower levels of blood cholesterol and heart disease than people elsewhere consuming a similar amount of total fat. This has led to the suggestion that we should concentrate on those cooking oils with relatively high levels of the monounsaturated fats, like olive oil and rapeseed oil. It is not, however, clear whether the monounsaturated fats have a positive beneficial effect on the heart or whether it is the lower proportion of saturated fat which is responsible. Or, indeed, whether most of the benefit is derived from the large amount of fresh fruit which the same people tend to eat. Whatever the explanation, there can be little doubt that the unsaturated fats of cooking oils are much healthier for us than the saturated fat of butter or lard, or the trans-fatty acids of margarine.

Sometimes you see vegetable oils described on the label as 'cold pressed'. What does that mean? 'Cold pressed' means that all of the oil has been obtained simply by pressing the seeds, without it being extracted by chemical means. It's a bit more expensive because less oil is obtained from the seeds than by extracting chemically, but it's more natural. It also has more of the original taste, and there is no danger of it being contaminated by the chemicals used in the other type of extraction process, so you may prefer it.

Don't Drown in Cooking Oil

But you don't want to overdo the cooking oil either, even though it is mostly unsaturated. Always use the least you can get away with. Also remember not to keep on reusing the same old oil, as with repeated use unpleasant chemicals can build up.

Now for the take-home message. For frying, use a small amount of fresh vegetable oil, preferably cold pressed; never butter or lard. Better still, don't fry. Grill, boil or microwave, or use non-stick frying pans instead. Then you won't add extra fat of any kind.

The Restaurant Goers' Survival Guide

Advice to all those planning to eat in a restaurant. Don't. Most restaurants are a hot pan of fat. No, I am being a bit unfair; there are some very good restaurants, but be selective. I can't offer any advice about what to eat in posh restaurants as I never go to them – can't afford it. All that will change, of course, once the money starts rolling in from the sales of this book! Anyway, getting back to business. The best supermarket and caravan site restaurants usually offer a few healthy choices – there are usually boiled potatoes and mixed veg to be had with your bridie or Cornish pasty. Then there is the ubiquitous baked potato with baked beans or tuna, and a side salad. Wonderfully cheap – even I can afford it – highly nutritious, and low in fat. Vegetarian restaurants offer a healthy selection if you can afford them, although even they often go heavy on the vegetable oil. Bar meals, though less romantic are often healthier than the food served up in the candlelit restaurant in the evening, and for a fraction of the price.

Most student and works canteens have improved a lot in recent years. The choice used to be between pie with chips, or pie without chips, or chips without pie, but most now boast a slightly more varied menu. Again, go for the boiled spuds and green veg and baked potatoes, and avoid the sticky desserts, and you won't go far wrong.

Fat Fast Food

Fast food in general is high in fat, but it varies enormously between outlets. A small burger – often referred to as a "quarter-pounder"- from the likes of Burger King, McDonald's and Wimpy will contain around 10g of fat, 4g of which is the bad saturated food. Those on sale elsewhere from independent outlets typically have twice as much fat, partly because they are bigger.

The worst fast food in terms of fat is doner kebabs. They contain on average 45g of fat, of which half is the bad saturated kind, so a single snack will force you over the daily sat fat limit. Fried chicken, whether from Kentucky or elsewhere, also tends to contain a lot of fat, a standard portion having about 30g (about 8g saturated). Fast cheese and tomato pizzas tend to be much lower in fat than most of the other fast food, typically containing about 5g in a slice (2g saturated).

OK, now what about the chips, French fries, call them what you will. In theory, the smaller the chip the higher the proportion of fat sticking to the surface, because as you will remember from your maths at school, small objects have relatively bigger surface areas than large ones. It also depends though on the kind of fat they are fried in and how long it has to soak into the surface and how much is drained off before serving it and, of course, the size of the bag. The smallest portions on offer in Burger King, McDonald's and Wimpy typically contain about 15g fat, nearly half of which is saturated (or hydrogenated trans-fatty acids). Independent outlets nearly always give you a bigger portion, so you end up with about 30g fat.

If you succumb to the temptations of the fast food restaurant, buy Little Macs rather than Big Macs and standard (i.e. small) portions of the fries (why can't they just call them chips like everyone else in Britain?). When buying chips from an independent outlet, if you see them coming in big bags, just buy one and share it between two of you. That's what I like about self-service restaurants, you can easily save money by sharing, especially if you've got a loaf of wholemeal bread cunningly concealed in your jacket pocket to bulk out your half of the meal. Whenever the opportunity of getting salad, vegetables, or baked beans with your fast food presents itself, take them to create a more balanced meal.

Nutritious Nuts

Fresh nuts were once, like turkeys, a special Christmas treat, but now they, too, are available from one country or another all the year round. Just look at the variety to be found on the shelves of most supermarkets – peanuts, almonds, hazelnuts, walnuts, cashew nuts, Brazil nuts. They're available either in their shells ready to do battle with the nutcrackers or shelled in plastic bags ready for eating.

But are nuts good for us? The hazel was one of the first trees to colonise Britain after the end of the Ice Age, and at various periods of history its nuts have formed a significant part of the diet. Not surprisingly, as nuts are very rich in protein. They have almost as much as meat and poultry. Coming from plants we might imagine them to be low in fat but in contrast to expectations, nuts contain more fat than almost anything else, more even than pork and beef. With typically between 40% and 70% by weight of fat, Mr and Mrs Fat-Tooth should consume them in moderation. Having said that, most people eat very few nuts and need not feel guilty about nibbling a few more.

But as nuts are from plants, doesn't that mean that most of their fat is polyunsaturated or monounsaturated, the kind that it is all right to eat, rather than the saturated fat of sausages and burgers which blocks up unsuspecting arteries?

Eat Nuts but don't be a Nutcase

The expectation that nuts contain healthy unsaturated fat proves to be correct, but with one big exception, and I mean big. A coconut contains forty-five times more of the sad saturated fat than healthy polyunsaturated. The same applies to the desiccated coconut sold in bags for sprinkling on cakes. By all means go ahead and hammer and chisel your way into the coconut you win at the fairground, but don't make them a regular part of your diet; not that you are likely to! The coconut is arguably the world's most dangerous plant food – ever been hit on the head by one falling a hundred feet from the top of a palm tree?

At the opposite healthy end of the spectrum, walnuts, hazelnuts and almonds have ten times more healthy unsaturated fat than sad saturated. Peanuts, with four times as much unsaturated as saturated, are somewhere in between. More fat is added if they are coated with chocolate.

A vicar visited one of his elderly parishioners in her home. Sitting on the settee, he picked up a peanut from a bowl on the coffee table. "Do you mind?" he asked.

"Not at all," she said. As they talked, the vicar absent-mindedly kept popping peanuts into his mouth until he noticed that the bowl was empty.

"Oh, I am so sorry, I got carried away there, I didn't notice how many I was eating," he apologised.

"Oh, that's all right," replied the lady, "you are welcome to them. Since I started having problems with my gums, I haven't been able to do more than suck the chocolate off them."

Sunflower seeds are a delicious alternative to nuts, and unlikely to have been sucked free of chocolate beforehand. They taste just like nuts but with a softer texture and, what is more, are incredibly cheap, about a third the cost of a similar weight of crisps.

A word of warning about nuts. Never eat mouldy nuts, especially not mouldy peanuts, as they can be contaminated with a kind of mould which produces alfatoxins, substances which are known to give rise to specific types of cancer when fed to animals. And of course you will need to avoid peanuts if you are one of the small proportion of the population allergic to them. Otherwise, apart from coconuts and mouldy peanuts and those sucked free of their chocolate by elderly ladies with gum problems, nuts are a good natural source of healthy unsaturated fats and deserve to be nibbled more frequently.

Where the Fats Hang Out

To summarise, there is very little fat in fruit and vegetables and that is mostly polyunsaturated so we can eat as much as we like without worrying about our fat intake. Notable exceptions are the avocado with 14 per cent fat and olives with 9 per cent! Cereal grains and their protégé breakfast cereals and wholemeal bread are low in fat, a miserly two per cent, and most of that is unsaturated and healthy.

Nuts contain a lot of fat, usually (except coconuts) mostly mono and polyunsaturated, and can be eaten in moderation but don't overdo them. Cooking oil and mayonnaise are highly concentrated sources of both polyunsaturated and monounsaturated fats and can be used in moderation, but again don't overdo them. So is margarine, but most brands are spoiled by hydrogenating them to produce trans-fatty acids.

Poultry and wild game, like rabbits and deer, contain about 5 per cent fat in all with roughly equal amounts of the three kinds – a third saturated, a third polyunsaturated and a third monounsaturated. In fish, too, most of the fat is unsaturated. These are the healthy foods, with more unsaturated fat than saturated, that we can eat plenty of.

In contrast, not only do pigs, sheep and cattle contain about 5 times as much fat as poultry and game, but much of the extra fat is saturated. Full-fat milk and cheese, butter and cream also have high levels of saturated fat relative to unsaturated. That is why, to avoid overdosing on saturated fat, they should only be eaten in moderation.

In a Nutshell

Have you got all of that? By far the most difficult chapter in the book this one. You might need to re-read it. Remember the sad saturated fats and horrible hydrogenated vegetable oils (sometimes called trans-fatty acids) are the bad guys which clog up your arteries if you eat too much of them. In contrast, the unsaturated fats are the good guys, especially the monounsaturated and Omega-3s. So keep down the amount of saturated fat you eat. If you use cooking oil, go for those high in monounsaturates like olive oil and rapeseed oil. Similarly, if you use margarine, go for those low in terrible trans-fatty acids, and high in monounsaturates. For Omega-3s, eat some oily fish or the occasional spoonful of cod liver oil. Although too much saturated fat is bad for us, a small amount of fat is needed to enable us to absorb the fat-soluble vitamins, A, E and D and various other goodies, so always make sure you include some fat in your diet. Low fat, not no fat!

Chapter 9

From Mum to the Udder:
Milk and Dairy Produce

Replace all of the Whole Milk you Drink with Semi-Skimmed (except for children under the age of two years)

Other species get all of their milk from their mother, yet we get most of ours from a four-legged beast we have never even met. Dairy cows of the twenty-first century are high-tech creatures. Specially bred for their milk yield, they can produce enough to fill around 15 one-litre cartons every day for up to ten months after calving.

Imagine you are standing in a parlour that is fitted with automatic milking machinery. The herdsman or herdswoman – see how politically correct I am (even though Microsoft Word puts a wavy red line under herdswoman to show that it doesn't recognise the existence of such a word, and suggests I change it to herdsman. Sorry, Bill!). As I was saying, the herdsperson standing in a pit in the centre of the herringbone parlour washes the udders of each group of cows as they enter through the gates and take up their positions, then attaches the teat cups to their teats.

The machine, operated by a vacuum pump, draws the milk from the udders in a gently sucking action that imitates that of a suckling calf. The milk flows from the teat cups into a container that measures the amount of milk taken from the cow. It then flows through some other pipes into a large refrigerated storage tank next door where it is kept cool until it is collected.

To You the Customer

A tanker will collect the cold milk later in the afternoon and take it to the company's dairy where technicians will test it for bacteria, check to make sure it does not contain too much antibiotic and other contaminants and measure the amount of fat and protein. The milk will then be heat treated to kill the micro-organisms that cause milk to turn sour, so that it lasts longer, and then packed in cartons.

So, after all this trouble has been taken to keep us supplied with fresh milk, free of harmful bacteria, is it a good, health-giving beverage, or is it slowly poisoning us?

The Virtues of Milk

Milk, as everyone knows, is rich in PVC. No, not plastic, but Protein, Vitamins and Calcium. It is also rich in vitamins A and D and riboflavin, and is a good source of the vegan's curse, B12. Because of this, milk has always enjoyed a very healthy image and people have been encouraged to drink it. During the Second World War, meat and other food were scarce and there was a fear that people might not be getting enough protein. Milk was the answer as it was a cheap source of protein and was produced on British farms. It was provided for all schoolchildren during the War and in 1944 an Education Act made free school milk compulsory.

More recently, however, its image has become tarnished as we have come to recognise the dangers of too much saturated fat. So, exactly how much fat does milk contain? Four per cent. That may not sound too alarming, but it soon adds up if we drink large amounts of milk. A pint of *full-fat* milk contains just over 20 grams of fat, about two thirds of it saturated, so a pint a day would take us two-thirds of the way towards our daily maximum saturated fat allowance of 20 grams.

So does this mean that we should stop drinking full-fat milk? Definitely, but with the emphasis on the *full-fat*. **Don't stop drinking milk.**

Out with the Full-Fat and in with the Semi-Skimmed

A simple solution is to switch to semi-skimmed milk which contains only half as much fat as whole milk. People have been changing to semi-skimmed milk since the early nineteen eighties, and it now accounts for more than half of the milk sold in our super-markets, a clear sign that people do care about what they eat and drink.

But what about the protein, sugar, calcium and vitamins? Won't we lose half of these as well when we switch to semi-skimmed milk? Not at all, that's the beauty of it. The process used for removing half of the fat leaves the protein, sugar and calcium intact. The levels of most of the vitamins stay the same too except for the fat soluble vitamins A and D. These are reduced by about two thirds, but as we saw in the chapter on vitamins, there are plenty of alternative sources of both of these vitamins. Some semi-skimmed milk is, in fact, fortified with vitamins A and D so that it contains as much as full-fat milk. Read that label.

And what about the energy? Half of the energy in full-fat milk comes from the sugar and protein, so removing half of the fat doesn't make that much difference. Milk, therefore, is still a healthy food and we can carry on drinking it but we should always make certain that the milk we are drinking is semi-skimmed. If you drink a lot of milk, say more than a pint a day, why not make the second and third pints skimmed milk, which contains hardly any fat at all.

Skimmed milk is as rich in protein, sugar, calcium and most of the vitamins as full-fat and semi-skimmed, and like them is excellent body-building stuff. What it lacks are vitamins A and D, which you can get a daily shot of by making the first pint of the day semi-skimmed or by nipping back to the vitamin chapter to find alternative sources.

If the daily pinta on your doorstep is still full-fat, do what Big Brother says and make the switch to semi-skimmed now.

That Means at School Too!

The expert advice is that up to the age of two years, children should continue to be given full-fat milk, but that by the age of five they should be drinking semi-skimmed. Make sure that the milk your children are getting at school is semi-skimmed not full-fat, or at least that they have a choice.

Sheep and Goat's Milk

Goat's milk and occasionally sheep's milk are available in some supermarkets, as are yoghurts made from them. Are they any better for us than cow's milk? Only for people who are allergic to cow's milk. On the plus side they tend to contain more vitamin D than cow's milk, but on the minus side they contain a lot more saturated fat, about half as much again. As the semi-skimmed and skimmed varieties are rarely available, we are as well sticking with cow's milk.

Soya Milk

This is not milk from a soy sheep, but a milk substitute made from soya beans which may be used by people allergic to cow's milk and by vegans. It has a similar amount of fat as semi-skimmed milk but most is unsaturated. It should state on the label whether the 'milk' is made from genetically modified soya, but don't bank on it.

Say Cheese

The problem with fresh milk, as you well know, is that it very soon goes off, so men and women of old devised a clever way of preserving it. They invented cheese making. The aim of this ancient art is to take all the nutrients from the milk and leave the water behind. The cheese is traditionally made by adding rennet, which comes from the digestive juices of a calf, to warm milk. This causes the milk to separate into the solid curds containing the nutrients and the liquid whey, which is drained off. Chymosin derived from genetically modified bacteria replaces the rennet nowadays in many vegetarian and other cheeses. The type of curd produced depends on the amount of rennet or chymosin used, and the quality and temperature of the milk. This, together with the different techniques for converting curd into cheese, determines the finished product. At the one extreme we have Cheddar, which is very hard, and at the other, cottage cheese, which is very soft. As a young friend pointed out the other day, there is one kind of cheese that is made backwards. Can you guess what it is? The answer is Edam. Think about it!

Out with the Full-Fat Cheese

Cheese contains roughly the same nutrients as milk, but drained of most of its water is much more concentrated so, as you can guess, that made from full-fat milk contains too much saturated fat and should be consumed with caution. A hard cheese like Cheddar is just over one third fat, that's even more than pork or beef, so to avoid over-dosing on saturated fat it is important to go easy on full-fat cheese. Edam has slightly less fat, about 25 per cent. Like the milk it is made from, cheese is a good source of first-class protein so we don't want to stop eating it from a nutritional point of view, apart from which it tastes good. So what do we do? There is a simple solution: switch to half-fat and cottage cheese.

In with the Half-Fat and Cottage Cheese

It goes without saying that cheese made from semi-skimmed or skimmed milk contains less fat. Made from skimmed milk, cottage cheese has only around 4% fat while still retaining all the protein and calcium of full-fat cheese. Cottage does taste somewhat different from harder cheeses though, so if it's the real cheesy taste you crave seek out the varieties made from semi-skimmed milk. These have less than half the fat of Cheddar, about 14 per cent, but just as much protein, calcium, vitamin B12 and riboflavin. Most supermarkets stock two or three kinds of half-fat cheese but be prepared to search for them as they tend to get lost amongst all the other, less healthy varieties. Supermarkets respond to demand, and as more and more of us opt for the half-fat cheeses they will gradually take over from the full-fat just as semi-skimmed milk has displaced full-fat milk and wholemeal bread is taking over from white bread.

Why buy full-fat cheese when the half-fat variety with the same amount of first-class protein, calcium and most of the vitamins is sitting right beside it on the same shelf?

Butter, the Ultimate in Sad Saturated Fat

Butter is solid fat, two thirds of it artery clogging, saturated fat. To make matters worse, most butter contains enough added salt to keep your garden path frost free in winter. And to think that butter once had a healthy image! If consumed at all, it should be taken in small doses only. One in ten people in England still use butter or lard for cooking and one in five spread butter or hard margarines (with a high proportion of saturated fat) on their bread. Why, when there are so many healthier alternatives?

But perhaps I am being a little unfair. Butter does contain calcium and vitamins A and D. But it is better by far to get these nutrients from semi-skimmed milk, half-fat cheese, and fish, or make the Vitamin A in our own bodies from the beta-carotene present in carrots and other vegetables. With far more protein and less fat, other dairy products are much more nutritious than butter.

Double Cream

Everything I had to say about butter applies equally to double cream. How anyone can spoil such a beautiful, healthy fruit as a strawberry by drowning it with dollops of artery-clogging saturated fat as they do at Wimbledon, I shall never know! Give me the strawberries; you can keep the cream toppings, whether singles or doubles. After changing from full-fat to semi-skimmed milk, not many of us are going to be so perverse as to buy cartons of double cream, but it is still on the supermarket shelves. Just ignore it and perhaps it will go away!

Yummy Yoghurt

Yoghurt is the dairy product you can eat between meals without increasing your saturated fat consumption. It is convenient and there is no problem in persuading children to eat it, but does it live up to its healthy image?

Yoghurt has a lot going for it. It is made by adding a culture of special, harmless bacteria to warm milk. This is kept warm for a few hours to allow the bacteria to multiply and convert the sugar in the milk into lactic acid, which partially curdles and thickens the milk and gives it its tangy taste. Being made from milk it a good source of first-class protein, calcium, vitamin D and other vitamins.

Bio yoghurts contain one or two extra types of bacteria which give these yoghurts a milder, less acidic taste. The bacteria added are usually *Bifidobacterium bifidum* and *Lactobacillus acidophilus,* which should be alive and present in their millions when the yoghurt is eaten. Even if we never eat yoghurt, these harmless bacteria are present naturally in our gut where they help to suppress the growth of harmful bacteria such as *Salmonella* and yeasts like *Candida*, the cause of thrush. It has therefore been suggested that ingesting these bacteria in yoghurt may be to the advantage of people whose natural inmates have been depleted by antibiotics or severe diarrhoea.

Despite being made from milk, most supermarket yoghurts usually described as 'low-fat' have only about a gram of fat in each 100ml, not enough to bother about, and many have as little as a tenth of a gram in a tub. Compare that with a typical small (33g) packet of crisps which will contain about 12 grams of fat, a hundred times as much, and you can see just how much healthier it is to get into the habit of having a yoghurt as a snack. The price is much the same too. Even yoghurts labelled as 'Thick and Creamy' often have no more than the 4 per cent fat, the same as full-fat milk. As we consume smaller volumes of yoghurt, that is not so bad as it might seem.

A 200-gram tub of a typical low-fat yoghurt actually contains as much energy as a packet of crisps, so it will keep us going for as long, secure in the knowledge that the energy is being derived, as it should be, from carbohydrate and protein, and not from saturated fat.

A word of warning though. You may find lurking around the shelves one or two brands often referred to as Greek-style yoghurts which have a lot more fat, typically around 10 per cent. Just over half of this will be saturated so a typical 150g pot will inflict on us around 7.5g of saturated fat. Natural Greek-style yoghurts are often sold in giant 500ml pots rubbing shoulders with pots of natural low-fat yoghurts, so beware. Watch out, too, for chocolate mousse. They may look innocent enough sitting there in their little plastic pots amongst the yoghurts, but they have even more fat than Greek-style yoghurts. Thirteen per cent, over half of it saturated, is typical of the little blighters, although lower fat options do appear on the shelves from time to time.

Natural low-fat yoghurt is pure fermented milk but flavoured yoghurts may contain all manner of things to add flavour, sweetness and texture, even sweets in plastic cartons at the top and plastic spoons. Sugar is one additive to look out for. The best yoghurts have no sugar beyond that naturally present in the milk, nor do they have any other additives. Many, however, while free of added sugar, do sport artificial sweeteners, flavourings, thickeners and other additives. Many yoghurts, particularly those meant to appeal to children, have about three level teaspoonfuls of sugar (15g) in each

150g pot, as well as flavourings, colourings and other additives, the identity of which will be revealed if we read that label!

Working on the premise that while large amounts of sugar are undesirable, large amounts of saturated fat may be deadly in the long term, a small amount of extra sugar in our yoghurt, as in our breakfast cereal, is perhaps an acceptable price to pay if it means that we and our children will actually eat the low-fat product.

Ice Cream: a Vice or Just Very Nice?

All of those plastic tubs of dairy ice cream and choc-ices piled up in the freezer are almost too tempting to resist. Shall we lean over and have a look, or shall I be a spoilsport and give you a kick in the shins or some other gentle reminder that ice cream is terribly bad for us as it contains far too much saturated fat and eggs?

That is partly true. Traditional ice cream does contain too much fat. Indeed anything called 'dairy' ice cream must contain at least 5 per cent milk fat – the average is actually nearly twice that. Luxury dairy ice creams typically contain 15 per cent or more milk fat, two thirds of it the harmful saturated kind, a luxury we can well do without! Just imagine a one-litre tub of luxury dairy ice cream has as much fat as four litres (around eight pints) of full-fat milk! No sane person would scoop down a litre in one go, but Mr and Mrs Fat-Tooth might. If they did, they would consume 100 grams of saturated fat at one sitting, five times the sensible daily allowance of 20 grams.

Luxury choc ices tend to have the most fat. Before feasting on them remember they may contain up to 24 per cent fat. So long as an ice cream does not proclaim itself as 'dairy' it can be made with vegetable fats, around a half of which are usually the saturated kind, a bit better than the two thirds of 'dairy' ice-cream, but still not good enough.

All is not lost, however, because as soon as we start rummaging through the freezer we will come across a number of low-fat ices which taste just as good as the high fat. These lower fat ices typically have around 4 per cent fat. Although that is as much as in the whole fat milk that I keep saying we should avoid, so long as we resist the temptation to scoff it by the pint and confine ourselves to the amount we would get in a cone from an ice cream vendor, let us by all means treat ourselves occasionally. You see, I'm not all bad.

Too Good to be True

Even better are the frozen desserts like Walls 'Too Good to be True' or some of the supermarkets' own brands. They look and taste very similar to conventional ice cream and as their names suggest have hardly any fat at all, less than half a gram in every hundred grams, not enough to bother about. A bigger helping of these would be permissible. All ice creams and frozen desserts, even Too Good to be True, contain a lot of sugar but, just this once, who cares!

Chapter 10

Eggs take a Beating

What with scares about them being contaminated with salmonella, and the realisation of the harmful effects of too much cholesterol, eggs really have taken a beating in recent years. A great pity that because eggs are one of the cheapest and most nutritious foods around. For just a few pence an egg provides six grams of protein and a good helping of vitamin A and B12, folate, riboflavin, thiamine and zinc. Not at all egg-spensive is it? Eggs are one of the few sources of B12 for vegetarians. The protein in eggs is every bit as nutritious as that in meat and fish and, as they are so easy to chew, they are an excellent source of protein for people with ill-fitting false teeth who have difficulty chewing meat or fish.

Eggs, because of their very special chemical and physical properties, are also the miracle ingredient of cooking and baking. They are used for thickening puddings, custards and sauces. They stabilise mayonnaise and salad dressings. They are used to glaze breads and biscuits. They bind ingredients in delicacies like meatloaf and lasagne, clarify soups, and help sponge cakes and soufflés to rise. How could we survive without them?

A single hen of one of the strains that have been specially bred to be prolific layers like the White Leghorn, can lay enough eggs to provide you with a fresh half-dozen carton almost every week of the year. Despite the scares, every few milliseconds, somewhere in Britain, a hen pops an egg. Billions are consumed each year.

More than One Way to Crack an Egg

Just as there is more than one way to crack an egg, so there is more than one way to keep a chicken to lay those eggs. Aware of the appalling conditions under which battery eggs are produced, many of us are prepared to pay the little extra for free-range eggs. But beware of misleading descriptions of eggs like 'farm fresh.' If the hens are free-range, 'free-range' they will be called. 'Barn eggs' also gives the impression of freedom, but such eggs are in fact obtained from hens kept indoors, often under dreadfully overcrowded conditions, but at least they are not caged, so it is a step in the right direction.

The Eggs in your Cake: Free-Range or Battery?

Alas, when we surreptitiously consume cake and other products made with eggs, we have no control over where the eggs come from, as their manufacturers virtually never reveal the source. This is surprising because to be able to say that their cake was made with free-range eggs – I doubt if at present they ever are, unless you know different – could be a big selling point.

Two women are eating their sandwiches at lunch break. "What have you got on your sandwich today," asks Hilda.

"Tongue," says Jane.

"Uh, I don't know how you could eat anything out of an animal's mouth," says Hilda.

"So what have you got on your sandwich?" asks Jane.

"Eggs," Hilda replies.

It's because of where eggs come from that they are likely to be contaminated with the intestinal bacteria, salmonella, so cook them well before eating. High temperatures kill salmonella.

What about Cholesterol?

Some people are put off buying eggs because of their fears about cholesterol. Few of us can fail to be aware by now that people with exceptionally high levels of cholesterol in their blood have a higher risk of developing heart disease. Although consuming large amounts of cholesterol does not necessarily increase blood levels, the evidence suggests that too much cholesterol in the diet, on top of the DIY cholesterol supplied by our livers, may increase the risk of heart disease in members of the Fat-Tooth Family, who also eat too much saturated fat.

More Whites: Less Cholesterol-Rich Yolks

However, there is no need for anyone to be put off buying eggs altogether because of concerns about cholesterol because, as all of the cholesterol is in the yolk, not eating the yolks is a simple way round the problem. Eat as many **cooked**, protein-packed whites as you like.

People might think you are eggcentric but who cares. If you have just two or three eggs a week, be a devil and eat the whole damned thing. The occasional yolk won't do you any harm and you will benefit from its vitamins. Whole eggs are a good source of vitamin B12 for people allergic to dairy products. But if you have eggs every day for breakfast and especially if your wife, eager to get her hands on the insurance money, gives you two eggs with your bacon, it might be wise to tuck into the protein-packed whites and leave at least one out of every two yolks for the cat. Now I am in trouble with cat lovers, the dog then, no, the bin, but what a waste. This policy of overt yolk avoidance becomes all the more important the more saturated fat you eat. As we shall see it's the combination of cholesterol and saturated fat that is the real killer.

All eggs, including roe, contain large doses of cholesterol – fish eggs being no exception. Duck eggs contain twice as much cholesterol as hen's eggs, not only for the obvious reason that they tend to be bigger, but also because they contain nearly twice as much cholesterol per 100 grams.

Beware the Hidden Cholesterol in Cakes and Pastries

It is obvious that bacon contains a lot of fat and we all know that eggs are a repository of cholesterol, so when Mr and Mrs Fat-Tooth tuck into an occasional breakfast of bacon and eggs they know what they are letting themselves in for. Not so obvious a source, however, are the many heavily processed foods in which fat and cholesterol lurk unseen. Most prominent amongst them is cake. It is all too easy to forget that cake, unless baked by an exceptionally health conscious cook, is made from the lethal combination of whole eggs and masses of saturated fat, and is as bad for us as regular bacon and eggs. Cakes: an acronym of cholesterol and killer saturates.

Where Cholesterol Lurks Unseen

Rich Sources	Milligrams of cholesterol in each 100g food
Eggs	
Whole chicken eggs	380 (all in the yolk, 190 mg in a grade 6 egg)
Whole duck eggs	680 (all in the yolk)
Omelette and quiche	140-360
Milk and dairy produce	
Full-fat milk	14 (about 80 mg in a pint)
Semi-skimmed milk	7 (about 40 mg in a pint)
Skimmed milk	2 (about 11 mg in a pint)
Double cream	130
Butter	230
Full-fat cheese	70 to 115 (e.g. Cheddar cheese 100)
Reduced fat cheese	43
Cottage cheese	13
Dairy vanilla ice cream	31
Meat and Fish	
Liver and Kidney	400
Most meats	Typically around 100
Sausages	50
Fish	Typically around 50
Cod and Herring roe	500 and 700
Beware the hidden cholesterol in:	
Chocolate digestives	50 (about 6mg per biscuit)
Plain digestives	40 (about 5mg per biscuit)
Shortbread	75
Cakes	Typically around 100

Non-Egg Cholesterol

Cholesterol is totally absent from cereals, fruit and vegetables and is found only in food originating from animals. One of the few foods that contains more cholesterol than eggs is brains, but few people eat brains nowadays owing to their disgusting taste and to concerns about BSE, the inappropriately-named 'mad cow disease'.

Liver and kidneys also contain as much cholesterol as the same weight of eggs, but liver of all kinds, including that of poultry, is such an excellent source of vitamin A, vitamin B12 and iron that despite its cholesterol it is still worth eating from time to time.

Butter, too, has nearly as much cholesterol as the same weight of eggs and masses of saturated fat to boot. All dairy products contain cholesterol. Semi-skimmed milk, however, has only half as much as full-fat milk and skimmed milk has even less. Similarly, half-fat cheese has only half as much cholesterol as full-fat, and cottage cheese has very little. Meat of all kinds, whether red meat, poultry or seafood, also contain a significant amount. The more meat and dairy products we eat, the wiser it is, therefore, to avoid the extra cholesterol in egg yolks and butter.

Meat from wild game like deer and rabbits and from poultry contains only one fifth as much fat as meat from the Fearsome Fat Three -pigs, sheep and cattle – so does the same apply to cholesterol? No such luck. Meat from wild game is as cholesterol-rich as that from domesticated animals.

Cholesterol plus Saturated Fat – the Lethal Combination

If that is the case, as our ancestors have been eating eggs and wild game for millions of years, why have we suddenly decided that cholesterol is bad for us?

As I have already indicated, it seems to be not so much the cholesterol by itself which is the problem but its combination with too much saturated fat. Our hunter-gatherer ancestors may have eaten the eggs of wild birds occasionally when they could get hold of them (presumably fertilised eggs with the developing chick inside them, yuk!), but they certainly would not have had fat bacon and eggs for breakfast every morning. Nor would they have stuffed themselves full of cake and pastry made from eggs and butter. So be warned!

Chapter 11

A Vegetarian Diet: the Pros and Cons

The following poem expresses poignantly the dilemmas faced by today's meat eaters. Composed by an anonymous bard, it first appeared on the walls of the gent's toilets in the Department of Molecular Biology at the University of Edinburgh (the boss was called Mary).

Mary had a little Lamb,
Its fleece was white as snow,
And everywhere that Mary went
That Lamb was sure to go.

Mary had a little Lamb,
The Farmer killed it dead,
And now it goes to school with her,
Between two pieces of bread.

Many of us keep cuddly animals as pets, and yet we continue to eat animals which are equally as cuddly and/or highly intelligent. Is it any wonder that so many people choose to abandon their old carnivorous way of life to become vegetarians? A vegetarian is an individual who has seen the light. He or she lives on a diet of vegetables and fruit, grains and pulses, nuts and seed and does not eat meat, poultry, fish, snails or other animals, nor any slaughter products like gelatine and animal fats. There are lots of different kinds of vegetarian with funny sounding names.

- A **lacto-ovo-vegetarian** eats both dairy products and eggs. This is the most common type of vegetarian diet and is an easy one to stay healthy on.
- A **vegan** is not an alien from the planet Vega, but a vegetarian who does not eat dairy products or eggs. Vegans have to think carefully about their diet in order to ensure that they are getting enough essential vitamins and first-class protein.
- A **fruitarian** is a vegan who eats very few processed or cooked foods. Their diet consists mainly of raw fruit, grains and nuts. Strict fruitarians believe that only plant products that can be eaten without killing the plant should be eaten. Fruitarians need to be nutrition experts in order to stay healthy. Not for the novice.

Vegetarianism is nothing particularly new or trendy. It's been around for a long time. The orthodox Hindus of India, for instance, for religious reasons cannot eat meat. They traditionally get their nutrition form chapati, a flat bread made from wheat, supplemented with dahl made from chick peas. This magic mixture, cereal and peas/beans, gives first-class protein. They also eat whatever fruit and vegetables they can get and, not being vegans, consume milk and dairy products.

Getting enough of the right protein building blocks is harder for vegetarians in parts of the world like Guatemala where the staple cereal is corn (or maize, whichever name you prefer). This is because corn, from which they make porridge and tortillas, contains less of certain essential amino acids than wheat or rice. To help make up for the deficiency in their cereal the Guatemalans consume large quantities of black beans. The magic mixture triumphs again.

An increasing number of people are turning to a vegetarian diet. Some do so because they don't like the idea of eating animals, or they disapprove of the conditions under which farm animals are kept. They may be concerned that in a world where so many people are starving, grains should be fed directly to people rather than by the wasteful indirect route via farm animals. They may see the environmental damage wrought by livestock rearing; a hectare of rainforest cleared of trees for raising cattle is relatively devoid of life – in making way for the brief life of the cow you deprive thousands of other animals of the chance of life. Others become vegetarians because they believe that a vegetarian diet is healthier than one containing meat.

One of the potential nutritional advantages to the Fat-Tooth Family of becoming vegetarians is that the new diet should contain less **saturated** fat. That's good news for the arteries and it's good news for the waistline. It's also good news for the local Oxfam shop if you have to swap all your clothes for a smaller size. Remember that fat has over twice as many calories to the gram as sugar and starch. As much of the saturated fat that meat eaters eat comes from meat and meat products, and as vegetarians do not eat meat, we might expect them to consume less fat. The problem is that some novice vegetarians compensate for not eating meat by eating and drinking more dairy produce to make sure that they obtain plenty of first-class animal protein. There is a potential danger in this in that they may overcompensate and end up drinking so much milk and eating so much cheese and butter that they end up consuming more saturated fat than their meat-eating cousins.

Vegetarians may continue to drink milk and to eat dairy produce but if, on becoming a vegetarian, you initially consume extra dairy produce make sure that it is of the low-fat variety – skimmed and semi-skimmed milk, half-fat cheese, low-fat yoghurt. Most vegetarians also eat eggs occasionally for their first-class protein, vitamins and iron, but, because of the high cholesterol content of the yolk, they should not eat too many. Eat as many cooked whites as you like for their protein.

A further advantage of a vegetarian lifestyle is that vegetarians tend to eat more fresh and frozen fruit and vegetables that are beneficial in themselves. Having said that, there is no particular reason why meat eaters should not do precisely the same. There are also an increasing number of people who are semi-vegetarian. They forego eating red meat but continue to eat fish and poultry. As you will remember, fish and poultry are healthy because, while they still contain lots of first-class protein, they have much less saturated fat. That's OK if your main reason for going vegetarian is for health benefits, and I suppose that even if your concern is for animal welfare it is still a big step in the right direction.

Become a DAB Hand at Identifying Sources of Vitamins D, A and B12

Most vitamins are found in plants as well as in animals and getting enough of them poses no problem for the vegetarian. Do you remember what the exceptions are? Yes, vitamins D, A and B12. Readymade vitamin A is found only in food of animal origin but as we can make it ourselves from the beta-carotene in vegetables, notably carrots, sweet peppers and green leafy vegetables, this is unlikely to cause any problems for vegetarians with access to plenty of fresh fruit and vegetables. As for vitamin D, although it is not found in plant foods it is made in our skins in response to ultraviolet light. We don't need to be sunbathing on a Mediterranean beach; having a good walk every day even in dullish weather is usually enough. During the winter, though, it's as well to take some fortified margarine, or milk or cheese.

That Damned Elusive B12

Vitamin B12 is more elusive as it occurs only in food of animal origin, yeast, seaweed and supplements. Vegetarians can obtain it from milk and the occasional egg yolk. Fortunately, skimmed and semi-skimmed milk contain just as much as full-fat. Vegans who avoid milk and eggs are best to get it from fortified foods like veggie burgers, and some breakfast cereals, and yeast extract. Vitamin B12 pops up in a few other unexpected places like Heinz spaghetti hoops, to which it is added as a supplement and, of course, it is present in seaweed.

Ironing Out the Iron Problem

Vegetarians must also make sure that they get enough iron. There is plenty in greens like spinach, but it is less easily absorbed from the intestines than the iron in meat. Read the labels of breakfast cereals and other processed foods to find out which are fortified with iron. Vitamin C helps iron to be absorbed from the intestines so keep drinking the pure orange juice.

Behold the Magic Mixture!

As I remarked earlier, some people imagine that to grow really big strong muscles you need to eat meat. Try telling that to your neighbourhood gorilla. In a vegetarian diet, the first-class protein in milk and dairy produce and in egg whites can compensate for that lost by not eating meat and poultry and fish. Even without eggs and milk, however, we can still, like vegetarian gorillas, obtain first-class protein from plants by mix and match.

As you know, in peas and beans, one of the building blocks for making proteins is in short supply. Cereals also tend to lack one of the building blocks, but the good news is that the one missing from cereals is different from that missing from peas and beans. So, hey presto! The magic mixture of cereals and peas/beans complement each other to provide all of the building blocks (amino acids) we need for making our own protein, for strong healthy, muscles that would do credit to a gorilla.

Chapter 12

Fishy Goings-On

Official recommendation: double the amount of oily fish you eat. That's really bad news for the fish and for the seabirds that feed on them.

White Fish

Fish is one of the healthiest of foods. High in first-class protein and low in calories and fat, white fish provides a perfect alternative to other sources of animal protein like beef. Cod and haddock tend to be fairly expensive owing to a reduction in stocks due to over fishing, but other slightly less familiar, but no less nutritious, kinds like coley, hake and whiting are often available at a lower price.

The familiar flatfish such as plaice and lemon sole, which live on the seabed, are as rich in protein, as low in fat and just as easy to prepare as their vertical relatives. They can be grilled or, better still, steamed between two plates over boiling water. If the same boiling water contains potatoes or rice this method is also super economical in fuel. Haddock can, of course, be bought smoked like the familiar Arbroath smokies, but smoke is nasty stuff, whether it's emanating from a tube of burning leaves in your mouth or a from a fire beneath a row of suspended fish or meat and you might prefer to avoid it.

Deep Sea Oil

Despite the fact that some of them have as much fat as the same weight of red meat, oily fish, such as trout, salmon, sardines, pilchards, herring, mackerel and tuna are an especially valuable addition to our diet. While you might think that all this fat would mean that they should be avoided, this is not the case at all because the fat in oily fish is mostly unsaturated fat, the healthy kind. More importantly, it includes those essential fatty acids we mentioned earlier, the ones that sound like a planet in a distant solar system – the Omega-3 – those that help protect against heart attacks by reducing the tendency of blood to clot and form blockages in diseased arteries.

Doctors often advise their patients following a heart attack to eat oily fish to help reduce their chances of having another, and much research is currently underway to work out the optimal amounts of different omega fatty acid supplements to prescribe.

Oily fish are also rich in two of the ACE vitamins, A and E, that are believed to help protect against the damage to the lining of the arteries that, over the decades, can eventually result in heart disease.

They are also rich in the sunshine vitamin D, so even if you missed the British summer — perhaps you were working that day — you can still get your vitamin D by eating fish. Fish oil, whether obtained by eating the whole fish or by pouring a spoonful of cod liver oil from a bottle, is one of the richest sources of vitamin D.

As you will have noticed, the bones of canned pilchards and salmon are always soft and chewy. Bingo! As well as containing vitamin D, they are also a useful source of calcium, a great combination as we need vitamin D to absorb calcium from our intestines.

Two of the oily fish, namely fresh salmon and trout, are, in real terms, much cheaper today than they were a few years ago as a result of the development of fish farming, now a major industry in many parts of watery Scotland. Most of the fresh salmon and trout in the shops are farmed rather than having been caught. There is lots of it and it's not too expensive. In the wild, stocks of salmon have been greatly depleted owing to over fishing using inappropriate methods, to pollution and to the blocking of the rivers up which the salmon need to swim back from the sea in order to reach the upstream spawning grounds where they were born. Is that right; do salmon get 'born' or are they 'hatched?' As the salmon said when it hit its head on a brick wall, "Damn!"

When a herring is put in brine, hung to dry and smoked for about five hours it becomes a kipper. Despite being subjected to such violent treatment, the kipper is still rich in essential fatty acids. You may wish to avoid kippers that have been artificially dyed with the browning agent FK. Personally, I prefer to avoid kippers altogether and go for fresh products as the smoke used to preserve fish, or bacon for that matter, contains many of the same nasty chemicals as cigarette smoke.

Shy Shellfish

Not really fish at all but crustaceans, related to the familiar woodlouse (or rollypolly as they call it in America). You are unlikely to find fresh shellfish in your local supermarket and will probably have to make do there with the bottled or canned varieties. For the real thing, abandon your trolley and paddle along to the fishmonger. Cockles and muscles and other shellfish, as well as the homeless crabs, lobsters, prawns and shrimps, are low in fat. They have a reputation for being high in cholesterol but it's generally no higher than in beef or poultry. Shrimps are an exception with cholesterol levels approaching those of liver. If you are anaemic, cockles and muscles are for you. Cockles, especially, are a very rich source of iron. Shellfish in general are a useful source of another essential mineral, iodine, especially important in parts of the world where soil levels are low. At various times in history, oysters and other shellfish have featured much more prominently in the British coastal diet than they do today.

Despite their excellent nutritional qualities, shellfish have a dodgey reputation, as they have sometimes been responsible for outbreaks of food poisoning. They have a nasty habit of accumulating toxins from polluted water, including heavy metals and the toxins produced by certain types of algae. Blooms of these algae are becoming common in Britain and elsewhere at certain times of the year, particularly where their growth is encouraged by a rich supply of nutrients in the shape of fertiliser draining off the fields and animal or human sewage. Always ensure, therefore, that you purchase your shellfish from a reliable source.

Fish Liver Oils

These are an exceptionally rich source of vitamins A and D and the Omega-3 essential fatty acids. An occasional spoonful during winter is a good way of topping up our levels of vitamin D when there is too little sunshine to power its manufacture in our skin.

Pointing the Finger

Much of the fish that children, and many adults, eat nowadays is in the form of fish fingers. Fish finger protein is just as good as that of fresh fish but the saturated fat in the batter tarnishes the fish's healthy image. The same goes for the fish you queue up for at the local chippy. You will need to have a good rummage through the freezer cabinets to hook those fish fingers with the lowest amounts of fat.

Fish in a Can

As one lion remarked to the other as they lay watching visitors drive through their safari park, "They say that canned are as good as fresh; if only we had a key we could find out."

Canned fish is excellent and very convenient for a quick snack. I always keep a few cans of mackerel in tangy tomato source in the drawer of my desk at work in case I feel peckish. Canned mackerel, sardines, pilchards and salmon have the same essential fatty acids, including the Omega-3, as the fresh fish. Sadly, in canning tuna fish (why do people say tuna "fish", they don't say lamb "mammal" or chicken "bird") the natural oils are drained off, drastically reducing the Omega-3s. These are replaced by vegetable oil or brine so that the nutritional value of canned tuna becomes more akin to that of white fish than of oily fish. If your fish are canned in brine, remember to return it to the sea before eating the fish.

Chapter 13

Cakes and Biscuits: the Enemy Within

Halve your Consumption of Cakes and Biscuits

It is horrifying the amount of fat Mr and Mrs Fat-Tooth eat in cakes and biscuits without even realising that they are eating it, especially if they count themselves amongst the one in three adult Brits who eat biscuits every day and the one in five who eat cake every day. It may be better for some people to avoid cake altogether, remember the old Chinese proverb, "a journey of a thousand calories begins with a single bite". Or was it miles and steps; anyway you get my drift.

Cakes (Cholesterol And Killer Saturates)

Take down a packet of cakes from the shelf and read that label. No, stop – put them back again; the temptation to trolley them might prove too great to resist. Take my word for it; most cakes conceal between 15 and 30 per cent fat. That's as much as in the same weight of pork. The fat composition of different cakes varies, but typically about a third will be the harmful saturated kind, more if it's a cream cake!

Combined with the cholesterol from the eggs added in their baking, all this saturated fat makes eating too much cake as bad for the arteries as daily bacon and eggs.

No, of course I am not suggesting you should never eat cake. By all means go ahead and have a slice of your birthday cake or Christmas cake, or a piece of your wedding cake if you get hitched. Seriously though, cake can be eaten occasionally as a special treat – no need to wait quite so long as your birthday between treats – but it is definitely not for filling up on. That is the job of high starch foods like vegetables, bread and pasta.

If the urge to buy cake becomes irresistible, all is not lost because, as always, there are lower fat options available, but to seek them out you will need to read that label and compare fat contents. Some brands of chocolate gateau, for instance, ooze a massive 20 per cent fat, others a modest 5 per cent, a fourfold difference in essentially the same product! At the lower end of the fat range, jam tarts and apple pies can be a good buy; brands are available containing around 13 per cent fat, of which little more than a quarter is the harmful saturated kind.

When you buy cakes from the display counter in a cake shop, naked and unlabelled – the cakes that is, not yourself – it is always wise to assume the worst; namely that they contain as much fat as pork, a high proportion of it artery-clogging saturated fat. Most do. A great pity because cakes that are baked in small cake shop bakeries and restaurants for selling the same day could just as well be made with a high proportion of unsaturated vegetable oil. Not that there is any need to use much fat at all, saturated or unsaturated, when making cakes. There are lots of delicious low-fat cake recipes around.

Bye Bye to Biscuits?

Mr and Mrs Fat-Tooth just love their biscuits, especially the chocolate digestives. Most biscuits conceal even more fat than cake, and a higher proportion of it the artery-clogging saturated variety. To get a feel for just how much fat biscuits contain, take down a packet of digestives from the shelf and slice it into four quarters, mentally of course, not with your penknife or you might fall out with the manager. Visualise one of those quarters as solid fat and you will get the right idea, because that is how much fat most biscuits contain, an incredible one quarter. That is one heck of a lot of fat in a product which millions of people eat every day.

Biscuit labels rarely state how much of the fat is sad saturated fat. In most brands it is around half, which no doubt explains the manufacturers' reticence. Shortbread biscuits are amongst the worst offenders with around 25 per cent fat, two thirds of it saturated. The fat in biscuits and cakes is the hidden fat I keep warning about. It is the worst kind in the sense that the Fat-Tooth Family can go on innocently shovelling it down, day after day, year after year, without even realising that it is on the shovel.

But do I see a glimmer of light on the horizon? As we cast our wary gaze over the biscuit shelves, labels proudly proclaiming: "a quarter less fat" attract our attention. Closer examination reveals that even after eliminating this quarter, the packet still contains around 21 per cent fat. Never mind, it is a step in the right direction. A bigger step, a stride in fact, has been taken by at least one company that now produces a range of biscuits down to half the fat of the standard kind. To my taste buds half-fat digestives taste even better than high fat, and they have the not inconsiderable advantage that they give you a breathing space in which to withdraw them from your tea before they become soggy and sink irretrievably to the bottom of the cup.

Half-fat Rich Tea biscuits set the standard in low-fat biscuits, having a modest 6 per cent fat overall, of which less than half is the sad saturated variety. Arrowroot biscuits and Scottish oatcakes also tend to be less fat-laden than ordinary digestives. Despite their typical 20 per cent fat in total, in some brands less than a quarter of it is saturated. Best of all are those crispy, biscuity, rice cakes that float on air and are virtually fat free.

So it is now possible for the aspiring Mr and Mrs Trim-Guy to lay their hands on a packet of biscuits which is not absurdly high in fat. But half a dozen brands out of the hundred or so stocked by a typical supermarket is just not good enough is it? It's comforting to know that by prudent selection we can continue to enjoy the odd biscuit or two with our cup of tea. Am I not generous! Even a nasty, higher fat biscuit can be nibbled occasionally but, like cake, biscuits should only be eaten once in a while, not daily, and definitely not be used for filling up on. That is the job of starchy vegetables, bread and cereals.

To become the Trim-Guys, you don't have to *stop* eating anything! It's all a question of balance. Healthy eating means getting the balance right, keeping down our consumption of the less healthy foods and tucking into more generous amounts of the healthy ones.

Chapter 14

Savoury Snacks and Sweet Temptations

✔ Adults: cut your consumption of crisps, snack bars and sweets by a third.

✔ Children: cut yours by a half!

That's the official government recommendation, not mine kids. I know, that's just the sort of thing you get when the people in authority are adults. Not fair is it!

Crispy Crisps

Crisps, what the Americans and French confusingly call chips, come in a bewildering variety of flavours. One thing they have in common is that the Fat-Tooths and their kids love 'em all.

Crisps have just about as much fat in them as the same weight of bacon. They are a prime example of how to convert a healthy, first-class food, full of starch, protein and vitamins – potatoes – into junk food. Potatoes are virtually fat free but they accumulate so much during processing that by the time they are transformed into crisps we end up with one part fat to two parts potato – not quite potato-free but getting there.

To be fair, in recent years a number of brands of crisps fried in unsaturated vegetable oil and with very little saturated fat have made it to the supermarket shelves. Most manufacturers and supermarket chains have also introduced varieties with about a third less total fat than their ordinary crisps. That is still an awful lot of fat, but it's a step in the right direction. If we must eat crisps, these are the ones to go for. Most of the dozens of corn and other cheap snacks that compete for shelf space with the crisps are also over one third fat, a third of that saturated, as well as the usual additions of salt, colourings and flavourings.

The pseudo-ethnic snacks in bigger than average packets printed to look like hessian bags, with pictures of Indian or Mexican farm labourers, offer another ray of hope despite their nauseating presentation. Although the hardworking locals depicted on the packet have certainly never tasted anything like them, some of the snacks, like Indian poppadoms, contain only half as much fat as crisps and almost all of it is unsaturated. The same goes for some kinds of pasta whirls. They are strong and spicy, really tasty if you like that sort of thing, again with only half as much fat as crisps and very little of it saturated.

Amongst the nominees for top prize for a low-fat snack is the Low-fat Snack Company for their Potato Crisp Waffles, baked instead of fried and with only one per cent fat. So we can still partake of a quick, crispy snack, so long as we read that label and watch what we are eating, and so long as we stick with the standard-sized bags.

At all costs, resist the deplorable trend towards the bigger bag. The 65 gram bag of lower fat crisps which replaces the typical 30g bag may tell us that it contains *two* servings and the 100 gram bag of pizza bread that it contains *four* servings, but how many of us have the will power to put down a packet of anything until we have finished it? Remember that Chinese proverb again, a journey of a thousand calories begins with a single bite. The healthier snack soon becomes unhealthy if we eat too much of it and we find ourselves in the absurd situation where we consume more fat by eating the big bag of lower fat crisps than by eating the small bag of high fat crisps.

We started off with modest 30g packets of crisps sold separately. Then they began selling them in packs of six, then twelve and even twenty or thirty; and now the trend is towards individual bags two or three times as big as the original. How long will it be before they start selling these in packs of six, twelve or twenty, too? Is it any wonder that crisps and chocolate bars have virtually become the staple diet of so many young and not so young people?

Are you a Chocoholic?

Are you a chocoholic? Chocolate is made from the "beans" of the cacao tree, which grows wild in the Americas. The botanical name for the cacao tree is *Theobroma*, which means "food of the gods". The beans, which grow inside leathery pods on the trunk and branches of the tree are creamy white, not the dark brown colour we associate with chocolate. It is not the sun that makes them go brown, but the action of bacteria. They are cut from the tree, removed from the pod and left for several days in bins for the bacteria to transform their colour and produce the fragrance of chocolate. Once they reach the factory they are roasted, and after removing the shells, ground into powder and melted. From bean to bar is a long complicated process, and the familiar chocolate bar is a fairly recent invention. Although people had been drinking chocolate for hundreds of years – it was introduced into Europe in the 1500s – it was not until the 1800s that crunchy solid chocolate caught on.

Now the typical supermarket of the third millennium stocks a hundred different kinds of horrible sticky snack bars full of sugar and fat and coated with treacle and chocolate. Then there are those chocolate bars and boxes of expensive fancy chocolates. How people can stuff themselves full of this junk I shall never know!

I thought that little outburst would increase my ranking in the popularity stakes! No, I would never be so optimistic as to expect you (or myself!) and the younger members of the family to stop eating chocolate and sweets altogether, but remember they should be eaten only as a special treat and not become their staple diet.

Thankfully, many supermarkets have now, to the delight of the parents of young children, removed sweets from their checkouts, and a few stores have taken the radical step of replacing the sweets with fresh fruit. But so much for the good news. At the same time as individual snack bars and packets of sweets are being banished from the checkouts it is becoming increasingly difficult for parents who wish to give their children the occasional treat to buy *individual* snack bars on the main shelves. Many supermarkets now sell them exclusively in packs of six or more: the crisp story all over again. Bulk marketing of fat-laden snack bars makes it even more difficult for parents to limit their children's consumption of them to a sensible level and is a trend to be deplored.

It is not only children who like chocolate, adults do too. Although men are not immune to its allure, it appears to appeal particularly to the female instincts. Many have publicly expressed the desire to bathe in it. Some women also express the view that chocolate is better than men. They argue that it is dark, rich and satisfying; is mentally stimulating; always smells good; and chocolate doesn't just think it is smooth. Chocolate satisfies every time, size really doesn't matter, and if it gets soft a few seconds in the refrigerator will make it hard again.

The UK title for the best selling chocolate bar was for many years held by Kit-Kat, it's narrow chocolate-coated fingers having an especially strong appeal. It began life in 1935 under the name of Chocolate Crisp, becoming Kit-Kat two years later. Today, however, it has several worthy competitors. Another old time favourite – the Mars Bar – was first sold in 1920 by the American, Frank Mars. Being a very concentrated source of energy it was supplied to GIs as part of their rations during the Second World War. Hill climbers and mountaineers often carry a few Mars bars with them for the same reason.

All chocolate bars are a concentrated source of energy, very useful when our reserves are limited, but when did you last go to war or even climb a mountain? Snack bars make it all too easy to consume large numbers of calories and huge amounts of saturated fat in the blinking of an eye. Kit-Kat is typical of most chocolate and snack bars in being one quarter fat, putting them firmly in the same league as bacon and biscuits. A single four-fingered bar contains about 250 calories and 13g of fat, and takes about two minutes to eat.

A few snack bars do have somewhat less fat. Mars bars and Milky Way have a third less than many of their competitors. That does not mean that they are low-fat. They still contain about 17 per cent, over half of it saturated.

Some manufacturers are still very naughty and fail to list the amount of fat on all of their wrappers, only on the outer packaging. Others do so, at least on occasions, in such small print that you need a magnifying glass to read it. Apparently men from Mars have better eyesight than we do!

Can I not find anything good to say about snack bars? Yes, snack bars are not entirely lacking in vitamins; they usually have a trace of most of the Bs. They also have a modicum of protein.

Want a snack bar that really is low in fat, then try Jordan's crunchy bars. Made with oats, dried apple, honey, hazelnuts, sesame seeds and sunflower seeds, to name just a few, they have a mere half a gram or so of saturated fat to the bar. If we must eat sticky snacks, that is the sort to go for. No, I don't have shares in the company.

Multicoloured Sweeties

Sweets, however, are about as vitamin and protein-free as you can get. These pellets of tooth-rotting sugar laced with colours and flavours have very little nutritional value apart from the energy in the sugar. But they can be tasty, and one point in their favour is that they are usually fat free. Well, that's something I suppose.

For young children sweets are often more than just something to eat, serving as a form of currency. 'Let's have a go on your computer and I'll give you a sweet.' Just as adults treat their friends to a pint or a coffee, children offer sweets. Forbidding children to eat sweets at all may, therefore, constitute an unwarranted interference in the development of social skills but sweet sucking should certainly not be encouraged in the home where healthier options like fresh fruit and breakfast cereals should always be readily available.

If the colourings in sweets cause you concern, take a look at the section headed 'Additives, the good the bad and the ugly'. Smarties boast an impressive list of artificial colourings. Uneaten, they make a handy paint box for children. The colourings are as follows: titanium dioxide, to give a white colour (yes, the same stuff that's added to brilliant white gloss paint) and carmoisine for red. Then there are Sunset Yellow, quinoline yellow, and brilliant blue, whose names speak for themselves. The remaining two colourings in Smarties are, in fact, natural substances, riboflavin (vitamin B2) to impart an orange-yellow colour, and cochineal, a red dye prepared from insects. The artificial azo dyes are often accused of causing hyperactivity in children, although a lot of children manage to be hyperactive quite well without their help.

It has become traditional to pick on poor old Smarties, but to be fair most sweets have colourings of one sort or another. Chewits, for instance, have just about as many artificial colourings as Smarties – Quinoline Yellow, Sunset Yellow, erythrosine (red) and Indigo Carmine (blue). Another old favourite, Rowntree's Fruit Pastilles, has its share; once more we are dazzled by Sunset Yellow and Indigo Carmine, while the red glow on this occasion is created with the aid of the azo dye, ponceau.

Tooth-Rotting Sugar

Tooth decay, as you know, is caused by colonies of bacteria which live on our teeth. The plaque, which gets painfully scraped away by the hygienist from hell, is made by the bacteria as a sort of bunker to protect themselves from bombardment by enzymes in saliva which might destroy them. Protected by the plaque, they lurk in crevices and produce acid that corrodes our teeth. They are able to make plaque more easily from sugars than from starch, and white sugar (sucrose) appears to be the best sugar of all as far as the bacteria are concerned.

What the bacteria really relish is a constant supply of sugar, so consuming one sweet snack after another or prolonged sucking of sweets without cleaning the teeth in between is ideal for them. Children should be encouraged to only eat sweet things occasionally and to clean their teeth afterwards to avoid the build up of plaque. Tooth decay starts very early in life. A recent nation-wide survey of young children was carried out by the British Association for the Study of Community Dentistry (a typical dentist's mouthful that). It showed that in the West of Scotland, where the water did not have added fluoride, children as young as five had on the average three decayed or filled teeth. At that rate virtually all of their teeth would be likely to suffer decay by their early teens. Top marks went to children in Bromsgrove, Redditch and Solihull where the average was one filling for every two children.

On your way to bed at night,
Brush your teeth shining bright.

Around the corner from the sweet counter you will come across a shelf full of tooth-brushes and toothpaste designed to undo the damage caused by the sweets. Despite the introduction of fluoride toothpaste, and the addition of one part per million fluoride to water supplies in many areas, tooth decay remains a major problem. Fluoride helps to strengthen growing teeth but will not provide complete protection against decay, and if we live in a fluoridated area it should not be seen as an excuse for poor dental hygiene. Fluoridation does not absolve us from the need to cut down on sugary snacks and to keep our teeth clean.

A thought to ponder. You probably drink tea or coffee, so if your local water supply has fluoride added you will receive a daily dose. Children, on the other hand, rarely drink tea or coffee, either they don't like it or, as it is a stimulant, we prefer not to encourage them to drink it. The sweeties make them hyperactive enough. Further-more, when did you last see a child drinking water directly from the tap? Most of what they drink comes in bottles, but from where? You may live in an area where the water contains added fluoride, but what if the lemonade and fruit juice drinks your children use to quench their thirst are produced in a part of the country where the water does not have added fluoride. Apart from the small volume of water remaining with boiled veg-etables, they will gain very little of the benefit of the local fluoridation.

In practice, as most water supplies now have fluoride added, the reverse is more likely to be the case. Even if fluoride is not added to your water supply, it could well be present in most of the water your children drink. This creates a dilemma for parents who are opposed to the mass medication imposed by the addition of fluoride to water supplies, while at the same time providing an opportunity for those who are in favour, but live in an area where it isn't added. If you are concerned one way or the other, just look at the label, find out the address of the company that produces it, give them a ring and ask if their water is fluoridated. The problem is that the sugar and carbonic acid in most fizzy drinks probably does as much harm to teeth as the fluoride does good.

If, as is preferable, the family's favourite drink is *pure* fruit juice it is not going to be easy to find out whether the soils of the plantation in South Africa or the USA or wherever the fruit was grown contains fluoride. You could do, but don't send me the telephone bill. In that case, fluoride toothpaste is the preferred option.

Sugar: Don't let it Distort your Diet

It is not only sweets that contain sugar. Manufacturers shovel it into all sorts of things – cakes and biscuits, sticky pudding, chocolate bars, even most breakfast cereals.

Sugar in sensible amounts is a perfectly acceptable part of a healthy diet. Many healthy foods, of which fresh fruit is a prime example, contain a lot of sugar. Fruit sugar is not quite the same as the pure white sugar beet or cane sugar you buy by the kilogram in bags, but even the odd spoonful of white sugar in your tea won't do you any harm. The problem is that ridiculously large amounts of sugar are poured into many foods and drinks. Unlike the cup of tea with its single spoonful, a can of coke

How Many Teaspoons?
One level teaspoon holds about 5g sugar,

Snacks	Number of teaspoons of sugar
Mars Bar (100g size)	13
Boiled sweets (100 g)	17
Chocolate digestive biscuits (4 biscuits)	4
Cake (a typical 100g slice)	8
Drinks	
Coca Cola (a 330ml can)	7
Pure orange juice (a large 330ml mug)	7
A cup of tea	It's up to you; aim for one or less
Breakfast cereals (one bowl of 50 g)	
Sugar Puffs	6
Frosties	4
Cornflakes	1
Weetabix	1
Shredded Wheat	1
Baked beans (one 205g can)	2.5
Canned fruit	
Fruit cocktail in juice (105g)	1.5
Fruit cocktail in syrup (105g)	3.0
Fresh fruit, without the skin.	Natural fruit sugar
Banana (100g)	4
Orange (160g)	2.5
Apple (100g)	2.5

contains about seven spoons of sugar. So do most kinds of non-diet fizzy drinks, which is why it is so important to go for the diet varieties. Many children's breakfast cereals, such as Frosties and Sugar Puffs, are plastered with sugar. There is a huge amount in most cakes and biscuits and sticky puddings. Sugar, as we have seen, is even added to baked beans.

The table below shows the amount of sugar in some popular snacks. In fruit and pure fruit juice all of the sugar is a natural part of the fruit and none will have been added. At the other extreme, in the fizzy drinks all of the sugar will have been added by the manufacturer. This table is just for fun. I am not suggesting you should always select your food according to its sugar content. The amount of fat and total calories are much more important considerations.

It makes sense to avoid foods and drinks that are obviously excessively sweet, but having said that, sweet things are all right for a special treat from time to time. I would never stop eating baked beans just because they contain sugar, as they are so nutritious otherwise.

Sugar the Temptress

Sugar is a naked white temptress who, with her overpowering appeal to the taste buds, can seduce us into eating all manner of unhealthy, highly processed, high fat, low vitamin foods, in which she appears, like cakes, biscuits and snack bars. Better by far to satisfy our lust for sweetness by tucking into lots of apples and pears, bananas, grapes and strawberries, and fresh fruit that provides us with vitamins, minerals and fibre along with the sugar, without inflicting upon us unwanted saturated fat and additives.

A Sour Look at Artificial Sweeteners

Artificial sweeteners are for the sweet-toothed who wish to reduce their sugar intake but cannot give up their craving for sweetness, even if the sweetness does taste very different from the sweetness of sugar. Manufacturers like sugar substitutes because they are cheaper than real sugar, and because much smaller amounts are required. Saccharin is 300 times sweeter than sugar, so only one three hundredth as much is needed, reducing transport and handling costs. The problem is that manufacturers add artificial sweeteners automatically to almost every diet and low calorie product on the market to replace the sweetness of the sugar that has been removed. As the range of products to which they are added increases, the sweeteners are being rammed in increasing amounts down the throats of those of us who can manage perfectly well without either sugar or artificial sweeteners.

As they turn up in more and more products and consumption increases, the question of safety becomes more urgent. Saccharin has been around for a century, but we are still not certain whether or not it is absolutely safe. Those suspicious of it point to experiments which showed that in enormous doses it can cause cancer in rats, but people who consume more saccharin than the average have not been shown to be more likely to get cancer. It is added to many soft drinks, canned foods, ice lollies, confectionery and so on.

Another popular sweetener, acesulfame-K, turns up in products as diverse as low calorie yoghurts and baked beans. About 200 times sweeter than sugar, it is more resistant to heat than saccharin and so can be used in products that undergo cooking.

First introduced into Britain in the mid-eighties, aspartame is about 180 times sweeter than sugar. It loses its sweetness on contact with heat and so is not suitable for cooking. It is made from amino acids which, as you know, are the building blocks of proteins. The two it contains are aspartic acid and phenylalanine. Because it contains phenlyalanine it needs to be avoided by the one child in 16,000 who suffers from the rare genetic condition known as phenylketonuria. Sufferers are unable to deal effectively with phenylalanine and become ill if they consume too much of it. Aspartame sweetens a wide variety of diet soft drinks and low calorie foods. Sold under the name of NutraSweet or Canderel it is also available in sachets for sweetening tea or coffee, to which it imparts its own unique taste. The recent Health Survey for England, found that only half of the men and one in four of the women interviewed added sugar to their tea, many of the remainder presumably using artificial sweeteners.

Is there a limit to how much of the artificial sweeteners we can safely consume and, if so, what is the limit? There is an organisation called the Committee on Toxicity that looks at additives like sweeteners and decides whether to set what they call an Acceptable Daily Intake. So how do the learned members of the committee decide what constitutes an acceptable daily intake? Firstly, they determine from the results of experiments placed before them the maximum amount that can be added to an animal's diet without causing an adverse effect. They then divide it by a hundred. It's about as Mickey Mouse as you can get, but as you can't do experiments of this kind on people, feeding them increasing doses until they keel over, that is about the best the committee can do under the circumstances.

Based on these calculations, the acceptable daily intake for a 60kg adult is 300mg of saccharin, 540mg of acesulfame and 2,400mg of aspartame. For a child weighing half as much, reduce these limits by a half.

This information is about as useful as knowing how many times the annual banana crop if laid end to end would encircle the globe, the reason being that we haven't a clue as to how much artificial sweetener we are consuming. If a product contains a sweetener the fact must be stated on the label but the manufacturer is not obliged to say how much of it there is, and so virtually never does.

I'm Sweet Enough

Manufacturers have this perverse notion that if they don't add sugar to their products they must add artificial sweeteners instead. Artificial sweeteners are a waste of space. They do nothing worthwhile. They don't kill bacteria or moulds, they don't prevent food from going rancid. All they do is give it a peculiar kind of sickly sweetness and encourage the sweet tooth. I for one don't want artificial sweeteners added to my 'healthy' baked beans or low-fat rice pudding any more than I want sugar. So, manufacturers of diet products read my lips: **we don't want the sugar in reduced sugar products automatically replaced by artificial sweeteners. Let the consumer decide.**

The Healthy Office Snack

For a low-fat, low calorie snack choose an apple or banana, perhaps with a slice of bread, or a yoghurt, and leave the crisps, biscuits and chocolate bars alone. The following table compares the calories in a few popular snacks. Willpower, willpower, that's all you need, willpower.

For an energy-rich drink complete with natural sugar and extra nutrients, drink semi-skimmed milk or pure fruit juice. If weight control is your main aim, tea, even with a spoonful of sugar, and the diet varieties of fizzy drinks may be for you, but take the more nutritious drinks from time to time as well. Tea and coffee are best drunk weak with just one spoonful of sugar. Make it yourself because, no matter how much you ask, other people will always make your tea the way *they* like it.

The Healthy Office Snack

Type of snack	Kcal in each portion	Grams of fat in each portion
High calorie munchies		
KitKat (48g bar)	240	12
Mars Bar (65g bar)	290	11
Four standard digestive biscuits	280	13
Ordinary crisps (30g bag)	160	11
Lower calorie munchies		
One medium slice of wholemeal bread	70	0.8
Four Trim rich tea biscuits	120	4
Potato Crisp waffles	100	Trace
Banana (160 g)	90	Trace
Apple (100 g)	40	Trace
Very low-fat natural yoghurt (120g pot)	60	Trace
Drinks (250ml glass)		
Semi-skimmed milk	120	4
Pure orange juice	110	Nil
Drinks (330ml can)		
Lucozade	250	Nil
Coke	140	Nil
Diet coke	1	Nil
Mug of tea (with 15mls semi-skimmed milk and one teaspoon (5g) of sugar	30	Trace

Chapter 15

Drinks: Fizzy, Hot and Intoxicating

The Cola Zone – Cans Of Lots of Additives

Most supermarkets stock around 50 different kinds of coloured and flavoured sugar dissolved in carbonated water. What makes one fizzy drink different from another is the cocktail of colourings and flavourings added to them. The diet varieties don't even contain the sugar, which is replaced by artificial sweeteners, and so are of no nutritional value whatsoever. We may as well just drink tap water. It's a lot cheaper. Odd isn't it that while some brands of washing up liquid contain real lemons, many brands of lemonade contain no lemons whatsoever. That said, a lot of people like the taste of fizzy drinks – and who doesn't enjoy the odd can of Coke or IronBru from time to time, so is there any harm in them? It depends on whether we look upon what we drink as an integral part of our diet, or just as an alternative to water to quench our thirst. So long as the colourings, flavourings and artificial sweeteners are not doing us any harm, then the diet varieties may be perfectly acceptable for those of us who are certain we are getting enough energy and vitamins from the food we eat and just want a pleasant way of quenching our thirst.

At the other end of the energy spectrum, the main contender for the title of The Most Fattening Fizzy Drink is Lucozade, weighing in with no less than 18 per cent sugar (mostly glucose). But as it is marketed as a source of energy for sick folk not up to taking solid food, and as an energy booster for athletes, we can hardly complain about its sugar content. Despite its traditional high-energy image, even some Lucozade varieties are now available *lite* with only half the usual amount of sugar.

Adopt a positive attitude in regard to drinks and look upon them as a nutritional opportunity, homing in on the vitamins and carbohydrate of the pure fruit juices and ignoring for the most part the fizzy varieties. Pure fruit juice contains about 10 per cent natural sugar. For people who need a fair amount of energy but may have small appetites, such as children and the elderly, this natural sugar is a welcome, easily consumed source of energy. If you want to wean your children off sugary/high fat snack bars and fatty crisps, but are afraid that in the process you may deprive them of valuable calories, pure fruit juice is the answer. It provides a rapid means of replacing the lost energy, with the added bonus of a daily shot of vitamin C.

Although pure fruit juice is the healthy shopper's drink of choice, obtaining energy from the white sugar in the non-diet varieties of fizzy drinks is arguably preferable to obtaining it from the saturated fat in snack bars and crisps. The odd can of fizzy drink *instead* of a snack bar or packet of crisps is not going to do us any harm, so long as we remember that, nutritionally, pure fruit juice is far superior and the drink to include in our staple diet. Ironically, owing to the mild laxative effect of pure fruit juice, if you suffer the curse of gastro-enteritis with an accompaniment of severe diarrhoea, a fizzy drink like 7-UP, which contains sugar but no fruit juice, is a better bet for replacing lost fluids. But get rid of the fizz first.

Why not give *pure* fruit juice a fizz for those who like their tongues tingled. Fizzy grape juice in what at first glance may be mistaken for wine bottles is, in fact, available in most supermarkets alongside the big cartons of pure juice. It's a bit more expensive than its non-fizzy relatives, but is still a good weekend, if not everyday, buy as well as being an excellent soft drink for putting the fizz into parties and receptions. Not that money is any object for fizzy drink fanatics. How many rich yuppies do you see buying their Cola or whatever in expensive, environmentally challenging aluminium cans, when they could buy the identical product in two-litre plastic bottles at half the cost per litre. Aluminium may be cool, but brass in your pocket is cooler.

Squashes for Diluting

While on the subject of fruit juices, we cannot allow those bottles of concentrated fruit juices for diluting with water to escape our attention. Some, like concentrated Ribena Blackcurrant Juice and Robinsons Lemon Barley, have been around for generations. Many people, particularly more mature folk who were encouraged to drink them as children, regard them as good, healthy drinks, an impression reinforced by their obligatory appearance on every hospital bedside cabinet in the land. But hospitals are unhealthy places, a lot of people die in them, so is that really a recommendation? Concentrated juices were, indeed, one of the few reliable, year-round sources of vitamin C before pure fruit juice became so readily available. They also had the advantage that because they were highly concentrated and contained preservatives, they would keep for a long time after being opened without the need for a refrigerator.

Despite the fact that nearly every home now has a 'fridge, squashes may still be tempting to those of us who have a long walk home or to the bus stop with our shopping. After all, one bottle of concentrate to be diluted with water at home is a lot easier to carry than five cartons of pure juice already at drinking strength. Unlike pure fruit juices, squashes tend to be coloured and flavoured, artificially sweetened and preserved. The better quality products like Ribena and Robinsons concentrated juices use natural flavourings and colourings like grape skin extracts and beta-carotene, but they still need the preservatives and usually artificial sweeteners. That's why they have found their niche in hospitals, not because they are especially healthy but because the preservatives prevent them going off in the constant high temperature of the ward. Shoppers without a car may consider investing in a taxi home from time to time to stock up on the heavy, long-lasting items like pure fruit juice and potatoes. That is unless you are blessed with a local supermarket like ours which, after you have selected your shopping, will box it and, for a modest charge, whiz it along to your home. Most of the larger supermarkets now have their own taxi ranks with taxis for the asking, while nearly all in-town and small supermarkets have a telephone - for those without a mobile - where you can call for a taxi.

Hot Caffeine

Mr Fat-Tooth likes his tea and coffee how he likes his women, warm and sweet. Neither tea nor coffee provides much in the way of nutrients until (semi-skimmed) milk and sugar are added to provide some protein and carbohydrate. Sugar is a source of carbohydrate we can well do without, although a single spoonful in three or four cups of tea or coffee a day (80 kcals) is nothing to get too upset about.

Coffee, tea and chocolate all contain caffeine. It is there because tea leaves, coffee beans and cacao beans naturally contain caffeine. How much caffeine a cup of tea or coffee contains depends on the variety and how strong it is. As a very rough guide, a typical cup of coffee contains about 100mg of caffeine and a cup of tea just under half as much. Plain chocolate has about 40mg of caffeine in every 100g.

In contrast to these natural sources of caffeine, soft drinks do not naturally contain caffeine; in these it is an additive. A can of cola has about 25mg caffeine, although some energy drinks have as much as 100mg. Caffeine is also found in many painkillers and cold remedies including most paracetamol and aspirin preparations.

Many people consume drinks containing caffeine because they say it makes them feel more alert, less tired, and improves their concentration. On the downside, it raises your blood pressure, and can give rise to muscle twitching and palpitations. It can make you anxious, irritable and prevent you from sleeping at night. If you drink large amounts of coffee you tend to became tolerant to its effects and need to drink more to produce the same effect. The lethal dose of caffeine is about 5 to 10g, so don't tip the whole pot into your mug!

Some people prefer decaffeinated drinks. The original coffee beans and tea leaves from which the decaffeinated beverage is made still contain caffeine – although genetically engineered caffeine-free varieties are being developed – but it is removed during processing.

A Nice Cup of Tea

A staggering 70,000 million cups of tea or thereabouts are drunk in Britain each year. Tea is not, however, purely a British tradition – it originated in China – but has long been drunk around the world where, over the centuries, it has probably helped save millions of lives. How so? Tea is made with boiling water and in parts of the world where cholera and typhus and other water-borne diseases are endemic – as they used to be in Britain – the boiling kills the bugs before they can produce an infection.

That reminds me of a notice I once saw in a foreign hotel: *"The water in this establishment is completely safe to drink. It has all been passed by the management."*

A word of advice. If you have young children around the house always make individual cups of tea rather than pots. Before the days of tea bags, hundreds of children were badly scalded each year as a result of grabbing the ends of tablecloths and pulling pots of boiling tea over themselves. Now that tea bags encourage us to make our tea in individual cups or mugs, the volume of tea children get over them is much smaller and, as it doesn't stay hot in a mug so long as a pot, it is less likely to cause serious harm. Not many doctors can claim to have prevented so much suffering as the inventor of the tea bag! Odd that despite having spent all that time watching kettles boil, wee Jimmy Watt never got round to inventing the tea bag.

Those little metal caskets with holes that you pop loose tea into and then suspend into the cup of water are actually more environmentally friendly than tea bags as they waste less paper. They are also easier to manipulate to get the tea at the strength you like it without getting your fingers burnt.

In more civilised regions it is the custom to drink tea neat and to savour, as one would wine, the delicate aromas of the different varieties before swallowing them. Tea drinkers in Britain usually commit the ultimate sin of destroying its subtle flavours by adding milk and sugar, the same people no doubt who are prepared to add water to a delicate Scotch malt whisky! I should talk! The only way I can stand the taste of whisky is to add a spoonful to a cup of tea (Gaelic whisky) and there is no way I can drink tea without adding milk to it!

Now for the one-million-pound question. (It used to be the 64,000-dollar question until 'Who Wants to be a Millionaire' hit our TV screens). Is banishing sugar from tea an effective means of weight control? If we find that a single spoonful of sugar adds enough sweetness to our cup (personally I'm down to half a teaspoonful), it is hardly worth bothering with artificial sweeteners as a spoonful (5g) only provides about 20 kcals. Seven cups a day would only add up to 140 kcals, less than the calories in two ordinary digestive biscuits.

Fizzy drink enthusiasts have much more of a problem as a single can of ordinary coke for example has the equivalent of seven spoonfuls of sugar, so we needn't feel too guilty about the single spoonful of sugar in our tea. The amount of milk people add to their tea varies enormously so it is difficult to generalise as to how many extra kcals are added in the milk, especially as it depends whether the milk is full-fat, semi-skimmed or skimmed. The helping of semi-skimmed milk in the plastic pots provided in restaurants (15ml) would provide a modest extra 7 kcals. The effort involved in getting the lid off the damn things probably expends more than that. Of course, you can always ask for tea without milk, and if the restaurant doesn't have milk you can have your tea or coffee without cream instead. Never add cream to your tea or coffee; that has far more calories and fat.

Tea has the reputation of being a good source of fluoride, which may help strengthen the teeth of those of us living in areas where the drinking water does not have fluoride added. Not all teas contain the same amount of fluoride; it will depend on the variety and whether it was grown in a part of the world where the soil is rich in fluoride.

Coffee

Coffee is also low in nutrients, apart from the vitamin niacin. While many people like its taste and aroma – I can't stand either, so its appeal is not universal – many also go for the powerful, addictive drug it contains.

Coffee was cultivated in the Yemen as early as the sixth century, where it was used as a food and thought to have medicinal properties. It was not until the thirteen hundreds that the complete process of extracting the bean from the fruit, drying, roasting and grinding, then brewing it in water arose to give us present-day liquid coffee. Arab coffee was very strong and drunk black. It was not until the early sixteen hundreds that people started adding sugar to it and getting addicted to the sugar as well as the coffee.

A British visitor to the region by the name of Thomas Biddulph wrote in 1600 about the extraordinary Arab addiction to coffee. "Their most common drink is coffa, which is a black kind of drink, made of a kind of pulse like pease... which being ground in the mill and boiled in water, they drink it as hot as they can suffer it, which they find to agree very well with them against the crudities (indigestion) . . . Some of them will also drink opium which maketh them forget themselves and talk idly of castles in the air, as though they saw visions and heard revelations."

The drinking of strong coffee is, therefore, the first step down the road of addiction to hard drugs and ultimate ruin, so watch out!

You know that you are drinking too much coffee when:

✔ You grind your coffee beans in your mouth.
✔ You sleep with your eyes open.
✔ You have to watch videos in fast forward.
✔ Your eyes stay open when you sneeze.
✔ You chew on other people's finger nails.
✔ You can jump-start your car without leads.
✔ You don't sweat, you percolate.
✔ You go to AA meetings just for the free coffee.
✔ You forget to unwrap chocolate bars before eating them.
✔ You've built a miniature city out of little plastic stirrers.
✔ People can test their batteries in your ears.
✔ Instant coffee takes too long.
✔ You don't even wait for the water to boil anymore.
✔ Your birthday is a national holiday in Brazil.
✔ You get drunk just so you can sober up.
✔ You can outlast the Energiser bunny.
✔ You don't get mad, you get steamed.
✔ You introduce your spouse as your coffeemate.
✔ You want to be cremated just so you can spend eternity in a coffee can.

Boiling Bedtime Drinks

As well as teas and coffee, don't forget the bedtime drinks, like Build-up powder, Complan, Horlicks and Ovaltine. They have the nutritional edge over coffee and tea in being fortified with vitamins D and B12. As these vitamins are not found naturally in cereals, fruit and vegetables, 'bed-time drinks' are a good thirst quencher at any time of the day for vegetarians and semi-vegetarians. As a bedtime drink they are preferable to tea, coffee and cocoa in that they are free of the stimulants that keep us awake.

Neither Fizzy, Hot, Nor Intoxicating

Nutritionally, the best drink of all is neither fizzy nor intoxicating; although it can be hot if really fresh. The drink I am referring to is semi-skimmed or skimmed milk. Milk is the only common drink that contains substantial amounts of protein, as well as carbohydrate, calcium and vitamin D and riboflavin. Children who refuse to drink pure milk may prefer to drink it in the form of milk shakes, choosing those varieties, of course, made from skimmed and semi-skimmed milk with natural colourings and flavourings. Limit the semi-skimmed to a pint or so a day to avoid consuming too much fat, but drink as much skimmed milk as you like.

Beauty is in the Eyes of the Beerholder

I have never quite understood why we always drink people's health and never eat it. Why should we not stand up and eat a stick of celery to someone's success?

Beer is a junk food. Lacking protein and with very few vitamins, it nevertheless contains an abundance of calories, from unfermented sugar and starch as well as from the alcohol itself. "I just can't understand it," says the pot-bellied Mr Fat-Tooth propping up the bar of the local hostelry, "I haven't eaten a thing again today and yet I keep putting on weight." What he doesn't fully appreciate is that one hundred grams of alcohol generates even more calories than the same weight of white sugar and almost as much as the same weight of fat.

The average Brit consumes around 20g of alcohol a day. That is equivalent to two pints of lager or two glasses of wine. This amount of alcohol alone provides about 140 kcal, and that doesn't include the carbohydrate. The average figure naturally conceals a wide variation, Mr Fat-Tooth probably drinks much more alcohol while many people drink none at all.

I DON'T UNDERSTAND THIS DIETING - I'VE HARDLY EATEN ANYTHING AGAIN TODAY, AND YET I KEEP PUTTING ON WEIGHT.

You're right, going down to the pub several nights a week and downing a few pints or sitting in front of the telly with half a dozen cans is as fattening as stuffing yourself full of cream cakes. Some men seem to prefer the company of beer to that of their wives. They will argue that a beer doesn't get jealous when you grab another beer; a beer won't get upset if you come home smelling of beer; a frigid beer is a good beer; you can have more than one beer and not feel guilty. The problem is that beer is more fattening than women. A typical can of beer or lager has around 135 kcal, as much as a dairy cream eclair! Down half a dozen cans and that's a massive 800 kcal. Extra strength lagers have twice as many calories per can.

Unfortunately cans of beer or bottles of any other alcoholic beverage for that matter rarely reveal exactly how many calories they contain. An exception to the rule are cans of no or low alcohol beers and lagers which do sometimes reveal their calorie count. It is, after all, very much in their interests to do so to tap into the weight watching as well as the breathalyser watching market. The label on a can of Tennants LA reveals an alcohol content of 80 kcal, which is typical of low alcohol lagers and little more than half that of ordinary lagers. You can get lower. Barbican, for instance, has about a third less calories than the average low alcohol lager.

As well as its calories, another disadvantage of beer is that it appears to contain female hormones; causing men, after a few drinks, to start driving like beginners and talking a load of nonsense.

Turning Up the Alcohol Content

Cider typically tends to have slightly more calories to the pint than beer or lager. Wine has more than twice as many calories as the same volume of beer but, as we tend to drink smaller volumes, that is not quite so alarming as it seems. A glass of wine holds about 90 kcal, always assuming that we drink our supermarket bottles of plonk in standard wine glasses (140ml) and not by the coffee mug! The calorie content varies with the wine; a *dry* white wine has about a third fewer calories than a *sweet* white wine, not that many people are going to alter their taste in wine to reduce their calorie intake.

Fortified wines have twice as many calories as the same volume of ordinary wine, but again, reducing the size of our glass by over a half to the pub measure of 50ml keeps the number of calories in check.

Whisky, gin and other spirits have nearly twice the calories of fortified wine. Liqueurs have even more calories than the same glass filled with fresh single cream.

The Boozer's Calorie Counter

What's Your Poison?	Kcal in each can or glass	Kcal in each 100 ml
Beers and lagers (440ml can)	136	31
Barbican low alcohol lager (440ml can)	55	12
Cider (440ml can)	176	40
Wine (140ml glass)	105	75
Low alcohol wine (140ml glass)	35	25
Fortified wines (50ml glass)	62	125
Spirits (25ml glass)	50	200
Liqueurs (25ml glass)	75	300

Pub measures are small but what about the amounts drunk in the secrecy of your own home? If you want to lose weight *and* stop drinking at the same time, join Alcoholics Anonymous and kill two birds with one stone! Should alcoholic drinks be universally condemned or do they have a part in a healthy diet? Until recently they stood accused, tried and convicted but then a number of research studies were published which seemed to suggest that a moderate intake of alcohol, like a glass of wine at a meal, helped to protect against heart attacks. The problem is that most people in Britain do not drink a glass of wine as part of a healthy Mediterranean type meal with fish and fresh fruit and vegetables. They are more likely to consume several pints of beer or lager in the pub to wash down their pie and chips. The greatest reduction in heart disease will come from an improvement in overall diet and an increase in exercise levels, not from a daily alcohol fix. An evening at the local leisure centre will have greater health benefits than one spent at the pub.

That is not to say that we should be completely teetotal. I am virtually a beer teetotaller but I like the odd glass of wine. The occasional alcoholic drink won't do us any harm, so long as we only drink because we are happy, never because we are miserable, and, it goes without saying, never when driving a bus or even a bicycle.

Chapter 16

Scan that Label!

Food labels can provide us with a fair amount of information about the food we are buying, substituting to some extent for the sniffing and feeling we indulge in when selecting fresh fruit and vegetables.

'Strawberry Flavour' – but where are the Strawberries?
The law says that the name of a product should not be misleading, but names will be misleading unless we understand the meaning of words and expressions used by manufacturers to describe their products. Take for example the use of the word 'flavour'. When this appears in the name of a product such as 'strawberry flavour yoghurt' it usually means that the product contains a cocktail of chemicals resembling the flavour of strawberries but no actual strawberries. There is no law which states that cheese and onion flavoured crisps need contain any cheese or onion, or strawberry flavoured yoghurt any strawberries. A product described as 'strawberry yoghurt' must, however, contain strawberries. The word 'flavour' is part of a magic incantation that makes real fruit disappear at a wave of the manufacturer's wand. Including 'flavour' on the label absolves the manufacturer from using the real thing.

Every Picture tells a Story
A picture of strawberries on the pot is a good indication that the yoghurt does indeed contain strawberries because pictures are not allowed to mislead and a yoghurt which derives its strawberry flavour from artificial flavourings rather than from strawberries is not permitted to show a picture of strawberries on the pot. Having said that it doesn't mean that there are necessarily very many strawberries in the pot, or even a single strawberry, maybe no more than a bit of one; maybe not even a big bit, just a small bit.

The name of a product should also tell us if the food has undergone any type of processing. Typical examples are smoked herring, dried apricots, UHT milk.

Low-fat: Lower than What?
Beware of wrappers which advertise a product as 'low-fat', as there is currently no law to say how low, 'low' has to be. There are, however, *voluntary* guidelines for manufacturers to follow if they make such a claim. According to one of the guidelines, a product described as 'low-fat' should have no more than 5 per cent by weight of fat.

'Reduced fat' is another expression to watch out for. A 'reduced fat' product should have no more than three-quarters of the fat of the regular product. Other wording such as 'lower fat' can mean almost anything. Comparative claims will, in any case, always mean different things depending on what kind of food we are talking about. For instance, a reduced fat margarine may contain only half as much fat as a comparable margarine, but still have ten times more than a reduced fat rice pudding, simply because there was so much more fat in the margarine than the rice pudding to begin with.

Fat-Free and X% Fat-Free

According to the voluntary guidelines, a product described as 'fat-free' should have no more than 0.15g of fat in every 100g. To confuse matters, a silly expression has come into widespread use in recent years. Many products are now labelled as '80% fat-free' or '90% fat-free', an expression clearly designed to give the impression that the product is healthy and low in fat. In fact, a product that is 90% fat-free still has 10% fat, which is an awful lot of fat. It needs to be 99% fat-free before you start to become impressed.

Reduced Sugar

Sugar claims should also be viewed with caution. Some manufacturers may put 're-duced sugar' on their product because it has less sugar than their own standard product, but this does not necessarily mean that it has less sugar that the standard product of another manufacturer. For example, I have come across 'reduced sugar' strawberry jams that actually contain more sugar than Robinson's regular strawberry jam. The only way to find out which is the best buy is to check out the nutritional information on the label rather than take the term 'reduced' at its face value.

Low and Reduced Calorie: compared with what?

Many products proclaim themselves to be 'low calorie'. Does this have any more meaning than 'low-fat'? Surprisingly, it does. Manufacturers are only allowed to describe a product as 'low calorie' if it has no more than 40 kcal in every 100g (3.5oz), about the same as a very low-fat yoghurt.

The expression 'reduced calorie' is that bit more ambiguous. Manufacturers can use it if their product contains less than 75 per cent of the calories of comparable products. But beware, don't be lulled into a false sense of security by reduced calorie claims so that you eat more of a product than you otherwise would, otherwise you may end up consuming more calories, not less. The same note of caution applies to reduced fat products. Don't use the low-fat tag as an excuse for eating more!

Throwing Light on 'Lite'

Another common expression popping up with increasing regularity all over the super-market, from the margarine to the biscuit counter, is 'light' or 'lite'. It too can mean almost anything, apart from the fact that the manufacturer never went to school. Firstly, what is the product lighter in? Seeing 'lite' written on a packet of digestive bis-cuits, a slimmer might well assume that they are lower in calories than standard bis-cuits and buy them. Read that label though and you may well find that they are lower in fat – which is good – but just as high in calories.

When a product is described as 'lite' it should mean that it is lighter in fat or calo-ries than a comparable product. Don't, however, take this as meaning that it is a healthy low-fat food. After all, a 'lite margarine' may be commendably lower in fat than ordinary margarine, but it will still be very high in fat compared to a 'lite yoghurt', which will have hardly any fat at all. For instance, a lite margarine may have 40 per cent compared with a lite yoghurt which has just a fraction of a gram in each tub.

Listing Ingredients

On packaged foods, it is the rule that ingredients must be listed in descending order of weight. If, therefore, the list on the side of a carton of a fruit juice drink reads: 'water, sugar, fruit juice, natural flavours', the drink consists mainly of water, followed by sugar, with fruit juice in third place. The flavourings are listed last as they are needed in only minute amounts.

Additives – the Rules

Additives must be stated in the list of ingredients, together with their function. If, for instance, potassium sorbate is present as a preservative it should be written on the label as "preservative – potassium sorbate" or if saccharin is added as an artificial sweetener it should be stated thus "artificial sweeteners – saccharin".

The information label enables us to avoid additives that we are not happy about and it is especially important to people who have allergies to particular additives such as the azo dyes used as colourings (or have children with such allergies). Manufacturers can provide either the full name of the additive or its E number. We will learn how to decipher the infamous E numbers later.

The Nutritional Information Table

Packed foods should have a nutrition information table containing four basic items of information. The first and most vital for the weight watcher is the number of calories in each 100g (3.5 oz) portion. The figure is nearly always given in both kJ and kcal. Ignore the kJ figure, as in Britain everyone measures their calories in kcals.

At least as important as the number of calories is the amount of fat, because it's fat, particularly saturated fat, that we all need to cut down on, even if we are trying to put on, rather than to lose, weight. The key bit of information we require is how much of the fat is the potentially harmful saturated kind, but some manufacturers still fail to reveal this.

The amount of protein is expressed as grams per 100 grams of product. So is the amount of carbohydrate. Some manufacturers also reveal what proportion of the carbohydrate is sugar. Most of the sugar in many products is added white sugar but remember that fruit and vegetables such as sweetcorn contain a lot of sugar of their own. Although manufacturers are not obliged to state in their nutrition information table how much sugar they have added to their product to tempt the sweet-toothed to buy it, we have a way of making them talk! Remember the obligatory list of ingredients where each ingredient has to be listed by descending order of weight. If, in a fruit juice drink, for instance, sugar features higher up the list than fruit juice, then you know that the drink contains more sugar than fruit juice.

The amount of each constituent is given in the nutrition information table as grams per 100 grams of product (including the weight of the water) regardless of the size of the can or packet. This enables us to compare one product with another. You may find it easier to visualise these figures as a percentage or fraction – 25g fat per 100g meaning that the product is 25 per cent, or one quarter, fat. For liquids, like milk, its fat content is given as grams per 100mls. Conveniently, this is much the same as grams per 100 grams, as a ml of milk conveniently weighs about a gram. Often though we just want to know how many calories there are in a packet of crisps or chocolate bar. As well as the amount in a 100 grams, some labels also tell us how much protein, carbohydrate and so on there is in a typical serving, or in the actual bar of chocolate or packet of crisps etc if it weighs less than a hundred grams.

Ever wondered what the big **e** stands for after the weight of the product? This indicates that the stated weight is the *average* quantity in the pack or can, but that the weight of individual packs may vary slightly from the average.

How Accurate is the Nutritional Information?

The nutritional information given on a packet looks pretty reliable. Often the amount of an ingredient is given in grams – 20.3g of fat for instance on a ready-made meal. Forget the 0.3g, there is too much variation between different samples of a product to say that the ready-made meal in your hand contains exactly 20.3g of fat. Stick to a good round number and reckon on around 20g. In reality it could very easily be between 15 and 25g, but the average in the samples that were measured happened to be 20.3g.

In regard to vitamin levels, remember they tend to fall with storage so who knows how close the actual vitamin level is to the one on the packet. Some manufacturers admit to putting several times the amount of vitamin given on the label into their produce to be on the safe side – so that the levels are always at least as high as they say. So remember that the values are for guidance only, don't put absolute faith in them.

Salt Levels Exposed

Knowing how much salt has been added to processed food is especially important for people who need to watch their blood pressure so that they can compare different brands of, say, baked beans to find the ones with the lowest amount. The provision of this information has recently become a legal requirement.

A high fibre content is also a good selling point, and most manufacturers now include the amount of fibre on cans of peas and beans to remind us that they have almost as much fibre as the same amount of high fibre breakfast cereals. They are, however, only obliged to provide this information if they make a claim like 'high fibre' for their product. Having made such a claim they must then back it up by revealing on the label just how much fibre it contains so that shoppers can decide for themselves if the claim is really justified. Nice to be both judge and jury isn't it?

Not many manufacturers yet provide a list of the main vitamins and minerals in their products unless, like breakfast cereals, they have been artificially fortified with them. This is a surprising failure to seize a marketing opportunity, as it could be very much in their interest to do so and would boost sales amongst shoppers on the look out for particular nutrients. For example, one well-known boil in the bag liver and onion meal, while providing the basics calorie, protein, fat and carbohydrate information in their standard nutrition table, fails to announce that it is one of the richest sources of vitamin B12, vitamin A, and readily absorbable iron around.

Where Nutritional Information is Conspicuous by its Absence

Food sold unwrapped such as freshly baked bread and cakes, meat and sweets is not obliged to carry a list of ingredients. It's a bit like pinning a medal to a swimmer, where would you put it? In theory a notice nearby should give some information about the product, including its main additives, but in practice such information is often lacking. Surprisingly, while bottles of fruit juice and squash carry a list of ingredients, bottles and cans of beer, lager and wine and spirits escape the requirement despite the fact that they frequently contain preservatives and colourings, an inconsistency that needs to be rectified. Some lagers and ciders, after all, contain the yellow dye tartrazine to which some people are allergic while others are coloured with caramel. Low alcohol beers and lagers may reveal the number of calories they contain, but that is about all they give away. The improved labelling of alcoholic drinks is long overdue.

Avoiding Food Poisoning: Date Marks

You can usually tell when native unprocessed food is past its prime by the smell and appearance, but how do you know when processed food has gone off? Well, if you see a price tag which reads 1s 6d that is a good indication. Another good sign is if all of the neighbourhood stray cats and dogs congregate within a minute of opening your 'fridge.

'Use before'

Processed food labels also provide a vital piece of information that helps us to avoid food poisoning, namely the 'use by' date. A 'use by' date is given on highly perishable foods such as meat and dairy products and ready prepared meals on which bacteria could grow and give us a nasty stomach ache. It is illegal to sell food after its 'use by' date. The 'use by' date assumes, however, that the food is stored at the correct temperature. We should always store the product according to the manufacturer's instructions and make sure that it is eaten by this date. If the label says that the product should be kept in the fridge at between 1 and 5 degrees C and gives the 1ˢᵗ April as the 'use by' date, if we don't have a 'fridge we should eat it as soon as possible. If we leave it until 1ˢᵗ April, it may by then have become a breeding ground for bugs.

'Best before'

Low risk food like digestive biscuits which can safely be kept for a longish period carry a 'Best before' date. Once this date has passed it doesn't mean that the food is necessarily dangerous but it may have passed its prime, the biscuits for instance may be soggy even before they reach the surface of the tea.

Scan That Label, Electronically!

Reading the list of ingredients is a bit of a pain for most of us. Think how much more of a chore it is for people who must avoid certain ingredients because they are allergic to them, or who wish to avoid certain things because they are vegetarians or have particular religious beliefs. But why should we have to take out our glasses in a desperate attempt to read the small print? This is the twenty-first century after all.

Do-it-yourself hand-held scanners have been around in certain supermarkets for years. Around the supermarket you go with your scanner, zapping the bar code to tot up the price of your goods. A fun device that helps you to keep track of how much you

are spending – great for students and authors on a low income – and saves you having to wait in a queue at the normal checkout.

Now suppose that the bar code were to contain a list of ingredients and other nutritional information. All you would have to do is to tell the scanner what you wanted to avoid, and as soon as you scanned something that contained the forbidden ingredient, the scanner would bleep out a warning. Great stuff, eh?

But how do you tell the scanner what you want to avoid? No problem. One method would be to key a code for the particular ingredient into the scanner once you picked it up in the supermarket. Another would be to have a personalised plastic card that you inserted into the scanner. This system would be great too for people wanting to cut down on fat. Just tell the scanner to automatically reject products with more than say five per cent fat, and leave the reading glasses at home. Of course, if it was something you really fancied, you could always override the scanner's decision whenever you liked.

You could even use the system for rejecting genetically modified food, or foods containing beef or whatever. Alternatively, you could use it for confirming that a product is low in salt, fat etc. Technically the system is pretty simple; but which supermarket is going to get there first. Watch this space.

Chapter 17

Another Additive, Another E

Why Process Food?

There are two main reasons for processing food. The first is to make it edible. You know how difficult the wholewheat grains glued onto the surface of some rolls are to chew and digest without losing a filling in the process. However, once ground into flour, mixed with water and yeast, and baked, they becomes readily palatable like the rest of the roll and less lucrative to the dental profession.

The second reason is to make it keep longer. In order to understand the importance of preserving food, cast your mind back to the Industrial Revolution when Britain had the misfortune of being the first country to become heavily industrialised. As more and more folk deserted the land to begin a new life in the cities, they had somehow to be fed. In those pre-tarmacadam and juggernaut days, when the distribution and transport systems were nowhere near as effective as they are today, it was not easy to get fresh food to the population in the cities before it went off. This created a very strong incentive to develop methods of preserving food – milk as cheese, fresh fruit as jam and so on. As most of the moulds and bacteria that spoil our food cannot grow in high concentrations of sugar and salt, more and more came to be added to all kinds of food so that it would keep longer. Sugar is used as a preservative in jam, but in most foods it is simply there to make them taste sweet.

Now, in the twenty-first century, with a steady stream of fresh fruit and vegetables being imported all year from around the world, kept fresh by refrigeration and rapidly distributed to every town and village in the land, the need for processed food is far less urgent than it used to be. Even crops grown in Britain, like potatoes and cabbages, are available fresh for much longer than they used to be owing to the development of high yielding varieties which mature at different times of the year, and of improved storage facilities and methods. So we are rarely short of even home-grown, fresh vegetables.

The same applies to dairy products. The development of supermoos that can produce a thousand gallons of milk in the ten months after giving birth to a calf means that abundant supplies of fresh milk are now available. It can be kept refrigerated on the farm while awaiting collection and transported into the heart of the cities while it is still fresh, preferably after having most of the fat skimmed off of course. Consequently there is no longer the same vital need for cheese or butter. There may still be a demand from cheese and butter fans but not the same need.

Technological developments that we now take for granted, like ultra heat treatment to kill off micro-organisms, and the sealed cardboard carton which prevents micro-organisms from subsequently entering until it is opened, mean that milk is now available all the year round, even in the most remote areas far from where it is produced. A constant supply of fruit juice is similarly available whatever the season.

Food processing started out as an essential means of getting food to the people in the cities and ensuring that everyone had something to eat in the winter when fresh food was scarce. There is nothing intrinsically wrong with processed food so long as it still serves a useful purpose. After all, the wholemeal bread I keep encouraging everyone to eat more of is processed flour, and I can recommend eating lots of breakfast cereals, frozen mixed vegetables and cans of oily fish. The processed foods lining the shelves of your local supermarket vary from the wholesome to products which are basically a mixture of colours and flavours with virtually no nutritional value at all.

Processed food can be good, bad or indifferent depending on the reason why it is processed, what is added during the processing, and its nutrient value after processing. When we start to get annoyed is when colourings, flavourings, sugar, salt and fat are added in unnecessarily large amounts during processing without serving any useful purpose, other than perhaps to boost sales amongst those customers who like the taste of the additives.

The only way of dealing with processed food is to read that label. Imagine your supermarket is a bookshop and browse before you buy.

Ready Prepared Meals for Busy Househusbands

The ready prepared meal is food processing taken to an extreme. A boon for busy househusbands, such meals are nevertheless a minefield. I came across a classic example in a major outlet recently – 'Salmon in a rich creamy sauce'. The healthiest of foods plastered with the most unhealthy. The Wimbledon strawberries and cream mentality revisited!

You can easily exceed your 20 gram per day limit of saturated fat by eating a single ready-made meal and the pastry in a ready-made pie. Read that label before parting with your money, and keep a wary eye on the fat and sugar content. The amount of fat per 100 grams stated on the packet may not at first sight seem too high, but remember that a helping of a ready-made meal is likely to be several hundred grams. Don't exceed the daily feed limit.

It's hopeless trying to advise what ready prepared meals to go for because the nutritional content of the same dish varies so enormously between brands. A macaroni cheese dish in one supermarket, for example, may have twice as much saturated fat as a macaroni cheese dish in the supermarket next door.

An advertising executive of a food company launching a new range of ready-made 'Sid's Square Meals' in a box had a brilliant idea. Much to the amusement of his colleagues, he decided to ask the Pope if, when delivering mass, he would replace the words "Give us this day our daily bread" with "Give us this day our daily Square Meal". In return the company would donate £200 million to the Catholic Church, half of its total advertising budget. So he rang the Pope and explained the proposition to His Holiness. The Pope listened, paused for a moment, and then was heard to turn to one of his Cardinals and ask, "When does our contract with Wholesome Bakeries run out?"

Be a Little Saucy

To make the ready-made meals more palatable you may wish to smother them with sauce. Tomato ketchup is still my favourite and with virtually no fat, lots of healthy tomatoes and, in the best brands, no additives or artificial colourings, it's definitely a best buy. Plaster it over your chips and you won't feel quite so guilty. If only the manufacturers would make it easier to get out of the bottle, they would sell a lot more. On the other hand, if tomato ketchup were made to flow gently from its bottle directly on to its intended target, widespread redundancies would sweep the dry cleaning industry. At the opposite end of the fat spectrum is mayonnaise which is about three quarters fat, albeit mostly unsaturated.

As for additives, while some sauces, like tomato ketchup, have none, others are loaded with them. As always, it is worth spending a little time reading that label to identify the best buy.

Additives: The Good, the Bad and the Ugly

Ideally additives should only be used if they confer some nutritional advantage on the food, the most laudable one being to preserve it. Colourings, however, serve no nutritionally useful purpose. On the contrary, they are often designed to dazzle us into eating nutritionally poor quality food such as sweets.

Cracking the E code

Do you find the list of additives on food packaging an incomprehensible jumble of meaningless names and numbers, mostly beginning with the letter E? If so, then this chapter is for you.

Let's start by deciphering these mysterious E numbers. The E numbers are a sort of universal language for use within the European Community. E110, for instance, is the code for a dye called Sunset Yellow which gives the yellow colour to yellow Smarties. French, German and other languages will all have their own words for Sunset Yellow,

E - lementary, my dear Watson...

but the E number stays the same; whether the Smarties are being eaten by children, enfants or kinder. Having a standard system of E numbers for permitted additives makes it easier to move foods from country to country within the European Community. British manufacturers are not obliged to use E numbers for goods destined for sale in Britain and a few make life easier for us by just giving the name of the additive.

Below I have produced a thumbnail sketch of some of the most common additives in use in Britain. When you see an E number you don't recognise, look it up and find out what it is and what it does, and whether or not it might be harmful. We will start with the colourings as these have the lowest E numbers.

Colourings

Many of the processed foods on the supermarket shelves contain colourings. Most are artificial colourings made by chemists, which seems strange when the countryside abounds with natural colours. Colourings are used for a variety of reasons – to replace colour lost during processing or storage, to create an illusion of freshness, to make otherwise boring products look more attractive, or to create 'new' products.

The natural colour of fruit and vegetables tends to be lost during the canning process owing to the high temperatures required to ensure that bacteria, especially the dreaded *Clostridium botulinum,* which is responsible for the potentially lethal form of food poisoning, botulism, are killed. Colours are therefore added to most canned food to replace that which has been lost; for example, a green dye is added to peas to make them look green instead of brown, the manufacturers believing that we wouldn't buy their peas if they were the wrong colour. Are they correct?

The problem with most natural colours is that they tend to fade with time. Anything stored in a clear glass bottle, like fruit squash, will lose its natural colour after it has been standing on the shelves for a while exposed to light. To make ageing fruit look young, the manufacturer of a bottle of squash, like the ageing Mr Fat-Tooth who dyes his greying hair black, uses colour-fast, artificial dyes.

Colourings and flavourings are much beloved by manufacturers because they enable them to create 'new' products. Adding different flavourings to, for example, potato crisps makes it possible to extend their range, the idea being that if they have five different flavours they will sell more crisps in total than if they only had one flavour. Similarly, if all of the sachets of blancmange in a box were of the same colour and flavour, customers might get bored, so they provide half a dozen different colours. Nutritionally, there is only one basic product but a colour here and a flavour there creates the illusion of variety and choice.

Back to Nature

Some colourings used in food production occur naturally. Those with the E numbers E160 to E163 are what make carrots more orange than oranges and give the red glow to red peppers, beetroot and so on. They are the beta-carotenes from which we can make vitamin A; and when used as colourings in the food industry are usually extracted from plants. With some other natural colourings, despite the fact that they occur naturally, it is more economical to make them artificially in the laboratory. The 'artificial substance' in this case is identical to the natural.

There are currently around 20 truly artificial colourings licensed for use in the UK. The two major groups of these artificial chemical dyes used in food colouring fall into two groups—the azo dyes and the coal tar dyes—which, as everyone knows, have been implicated in causing allergies and hyperactivity in children. Having said that, I have tried Smarties and they don't do a thing for me! So let us go through the list and see what we have. If you want to play about with coal tar dyes they can be bought in cute little bottles as food colourings on the home baking section. Amongst those you can buy are erythrosine (pink-red); carmosine (blue); and a mixture of tartrazine (yellow), Sunset Yellow, and ponceau (red) which together go by the name of Egg Yellow. They are great for giving your pumpkin a colourful glow at Halloween, but most people would certainly think twice before adding them to food that is to be eaten.

Baby foods are only allowed to contain natural colourings like carotene and riboflavin which double as vitamins. The only way to be sure of avoiding artificial colourings, therefore, is to eat nothing but baby food! Don't do it; I am just joking! To get us into a good mood, let us start off with two natural orange-yellow colourings.

Orange and Yellow, Nature's Way

Curcumin (E100) is a natural orange-yellow colouring extracted, not as might be thought from cucumbers, but from a tropical plant known as turmeric. It restores the yellow colour to butter, processed cheese and margarine, as well as being found in ice cream, fish fingers, curry powder and savoury rice. Another orange-yellow colouring is riboflavin (E101), our old friend vitamin B2. Hi, there! As well as being used as a vitamin supplement in breakfast cereals, it is added to sauces and processed cheeses to impart an orange-yellow colour.

Yelling at the Yucky Yellows

Now for the infamous azo dyes. In individuals allergic to them the azo dyes can produce skin irritation, symptoms reminiscent of hay fever, breathing difficulties, blurred vision and purple patches on the skin. Those who are sensitive to aspirin, or who suffer from asthma or eczema seem to be most at risk. Azo dyes are also suspected of causing hyperactivity in children. They are easy to spot from their E numbers as they all lie between E102 and E155.

Tartrazine (E102), the best known of the azo dyes, imparts the yellow colour to a wide range of products including biscuits, brown sauce, cakes, chewing gum, custard powder, fish fingers, fizzy drinks, fruit squash, jellies, and tinned vegetables to name but a few.

Sunset Yellow (E110) is another azo dye used to yellow up a wide variety of products while Quinoline Yellow (E104) is a coal tar used to give a greenish-yellow hue. It, too, has been blamed for hyperactivity in children.

Seeing Red

The first dye in our little red book is a natural colouring. Prepared from insects, cochineal (E120) is expensive to produce, so is not widely used, but is encountered in some alcoholic drinks, biscuits, cakes and icing. As it is derived from insects, insect-lovers may wish to avoid it.

The next three reds are azo dyes. The purple-red amaranth (E123) is one of the most widely used colourings and is to be found in products such as cakes, fruit squash, ice-cream, medicines and soup. Although banned in America, ponceau 4R (E124) and Red 2G (E128) are widely used to colour foods red in the UK.

Erythrosine (E127) is a coal tar dye used to colour foods pink or red. It was once more popular, but because it contains iodine, which, though an essential element, could in large amounts, affect the thyroid gland of children, its use in Britain is now confined mainly to glacé and cocktail cherries and Scotch eggs.

Getting the Blues
We have two true blues, both coal tar dyes that can produce allergic reactions in susceptible individuals and have been associated with hyperactivity in children. Patent Blue (E131) and Indigo Carmine (E132) are used for imparting a blue colour to a variety of products.

Turning Green
Brilliant Blue FCF (E133) is a synthetic blue coal tar dye frequently blended with the yellow dye tartrazine to generate various shades of green. It is added to some fizzy drinks and is used in an effort to reproduce in mint sauce and canned processed peas the natural green colour they lost during processing, although the resultant green is typically closer to that of the peas on the label than to the green of fresh peas. It is banned in most European countries. The natural green of our field and hedgerows is due to chlorophyll (E140) and chlorophyllins (E141). After extracting them from plants, they are added to, for instance, ice cream and soups.

The Rich Dark Brown Look of Chocolate and Gravy
The food painter is able to recreate this effect using caramel (E150). Large amounts of caramel are used in soft drinks, especially cola, and it is added to some beers, meat products and soups. To create the impression that their chocolate biscuits are brimming over with chocolate some manufacturers use caramel blended with amaranth to give a rich chocolate appearance. Similarly, to give the impression that they are bulging at the seams with meat, sausage casings may be dipped in caramel to obtain the desired colour. Some brown bread is simply white bread with caramel added to make it look brown.

Black PN (E151) is an artificial purple-black coal tar dye that is added to brown sauce, chocolate mousse and gravy. Carbon Black (E153) is produced from burnt plant material. It is banned in America owing to fears that handling the dye during manufacture could cause skin cancer. What then is it likely to do to you if you actually eat it? It is used to blacken chocolate-flavoured foods, jam and liquorice.

Brown FK (E154) is an artificial, yellow-brown, coal tar dye. Manufacturers add it to kippers and other smoked fish and gravy, and to impart a browned look to cooked chicken. It is banned in America and some European countries. Brown HT (E155) is an artificial brown coal tar dye added to some chocolate-flavoured foods. It, too, is banned in America and some European countries.

Back to Nature
As we have established, not all colourings are artificial dyes. Some are extracted natu-

rally from plants. Carotenes (E160(a)) are members of the family of our old friend beta-carotene which, as you know, our bodies can convert into vitamin A. They give the yellow colour to carrots, peppers, tomatoes and other deeply coloured vegetables. The range of products to which they are added include custard, margarine, processed cheese, rice pudding and salad dressing. Annatto, bixin and norbixin (E160(b)) are the various aliases of a yellow colouring made from the seed pods of the annatto tree. It is often used as a safer alternative to tartrazine. It is added to cheese, custard, ice cream, fish fingers and salad cream.

Natural colourings are now being more widely used in children's drinks and other foods as an alternative to the coal tar dyes. Take, for example, a typical range of milk drinks. To give the banana-flavoured one a yellowish colour, the manufacturers might add the natural colourings turmeric and annato; to give the strawberry flavour a reddish appearance, they could add the natural dye carmine (derived from cochineal); while to give the chocolate flavour a chocolate colour they might use the real thing, cocoa powder. Natural colourings such as these are a definite improvement on the synthetic colours used previously.

Preservatives

As preservatives have a practical function, slowing down the growth of moulds, fungi and bacteria that would otherwise cause our food to go off, their addition is more morally defensible than that of colourings. Even more importantly, they help to prevent harmful bacteria that cause food poisoning from growing on our food. The most serious form of food poisoning is botulism, which is caused by an organism called *Clostridium botulinum*. If allowed to grow on food it produces a very dangerous toxin, which remains deadly even if the food is subsequently heated to a high enough temperature to kill the bacteria. Preservatives are essential, therefore, if we are to continue to enjoy certain kinds of food. On the minus side, some can provoke allergies, and there are concerns about the long-term safety of some of them. Preservatives are easy to spot on the list of E numbers because they all lie between E200 and E297.

The Dreaded Botulism

Potassium nitrite (E249) and sodium nitrite (E250) are artificially produced preservatives used as curing agents for meat. Their most important function is to prevent the growth of the bacterium *Clostridium botulinum*, the cause of botulism, that most serious form of food poisoning. They are used in meat products such as pork pies and sausages. There is some evidence that they could react in the stomach with other chemicals called amines to produce new chemicals that might increase the risk of cancer. They are banned from food produced specifically for babies. Sodium nitrate (E251) and potassium nitrate (E252) have much the same uses as the nitrites, and can be converted into them in our bodies, so the health risks are also similar.

Mould Busters

Sorbic acid and sorbates (E200-E 203) occur naturally in some fruit and berries, but that used by the food industry is usually produced synthetically. It slows down the growth of moulds and yeasts and is added to a wide variety of foods including cake, cheese spread, frozen pizza, fruit pie, soft drinks, cider and wine. Benzoic acid and benzoates (E210- E213) and hydroxybenzoates (E214-E219) are used to prevent the growth of bacteria and are also effective against some moulds. You will find them added to a wide variety of foods, particularly those that contain fruit, like jam, pie filling, pickles, salad cream and soft drinks.

As well as being a major contributor to acid rain when emanating from power stations, sulphur dioxide (E220) is one of the most widely used food additives. It acts as a fungicide to prevent fruit from going mouldy; is used to prevent cut fruit from going brown; as an antioxidant to prevent fats and oils from turning rancid; and as a bleaching agent for flour. So versatile a character is difficult to avoid. It turns up in alcoholic drinks, desserts, jams and marmalade, jellies, fruit juices, pickles, dried fruit, soups, spices and vegetables, to name just a few.

Sulphites and metabisulphites (E221-E227) are used as a preservative; to sterilise equipment; as an antioxidant; and to slow down the browning process in apples and potatoes. They are to be found in alcoholic drinks, frozen chips, frozen seafood, fruit juice, orange squash and pickles.

A group of E numbers that you are unlikely to find on labels are those of the biphenyls (E230-E233) as they are used to prevent the growth of moulds on the *outside* of citrus fruit. They are either applied directly to the skin or to the paper that is used for wrapping them. If you intend using the skin of citrus fruit in a recipe, wash it in detergent first and then rinse it thoroughly to get rid of the biphenyls.

A Nice One, Nisin

Nisin (E234) is an antibiotic produced by a strain of *Streptococcus*. Like many bacteria and moulds, the *Streptococcus* bacterium produces antibiotics to kill or slow down the growth of other kinds of bacteria and moulds to give it that competitive edge. Some of the antibiotics, like penicillin from the bread mould *Penicillium*, have been exploited by medical science. It is remarkable to think that there are battles between opposing groups of micro-organisms armed with chemical weapons raging on a typical slice of mouldy bread! Nicin is produced naturally by the micro-organisms in some cheeses and may be added as a preservative to other cheeses and cheese spreads and some canned foods.

Some More Natural Anti-Mould Weaponry

A wide range of substances are added to food to prevent moulds and bacteria from spoiling it. They include acetic acid (E260), the scientific name for vinegar, used as we all know in pickles. Others are potassium acetate (E261), a preservative used in frozen vegetables and bread; sodium dihydrogen acetate (E262); calcium acetate (E263); lactic acid (E270); propionic acid and propionates (E280-E283). Bread is a common meeting ground for these preservatives, which collaborate to prevent it from going mouldy. All of these substances occur naturally in our bodies and adding them to food is unlikely to do us any harm so long as the quantities used are not excessive.

Present naturally in the air we breathe, carbon dioxide (E290), as well as putting the fizz into fizzy drinks, is also used as a preservative. Malic acid (E296) is used both to regulate acidity in foods and as a flavouring. Another acid regulator is fumaric acid (E297).

No More Rancid Fats and Oils: Free-Radical Busting Antioxidants

In contact with the oxygen of the air, fats and oils soon become rancid. Antioxidants are substances which help to prevent this from happening and also slow down the rate at which fat soluble vitamins in food are destroyed.

You may have noticed the term 'ascorbic acid' written on bread labels or powdered milk cartons and meat products. Ascorbic acid (E300-E304) is the scientific name for our old friend, vitamin C. This is, therefore, an extremely natural additive. It is recruited here for its antioxidant properties rather than as an intentional vitamin supplementation. Better known as vitamin E, the tocopherols (E306-E309) are also commonly used as a natural antioxidant in meat pies and vegetable fats and oils.

Not so natural are the gallates (E310 to E312). These are purely synthetic antioxidants. They are banned from food prepared specifically for babies but used in vegetable oils, margarine, instant mashed potato and some breakfast cereals. Butylated hydroxyanisole (E320) and butylated hydroxytoluene (E321) are other synthetic antioxidants commonly added to margarine, cooking fats and vegetable oil and to fatty foods like chips and crisps. They are used in a wide range of foods from cheese spreads to biscuits. Citric acid is often used with them to promote their action. They can cause an allergic reaction in people sensitive to them, and are banned from foods prepared specifically for babies.

Emulsifiers, Stabilisers, Thickening Agents and Sequestrants

As this versatile troop of additives is usually listed on labels by name rather than by rank and E number, I will avoid confusing the issue by burdening you with even more E numbers that you are hardly ever likely to come across. A brief word about what these substances do may not go amiss. Emulsifiers are used to mix water and fats or oils together into an emulsion to make them seem creamy. A familiar example is the use of an egg to make a mayonnaise or to bind a sauce, when the lethicin in the egg is acting as an emulsifier. Like lethicin, many emulsifiers are natural substances, well sort of natural – lethicin as well as being present in eggs can also be extracted from high-lethicin, genetically modified crops.

The purpose of stabilisers is to keep the emulsified water and fats together, counteracting their natural tendency to separate. Emulsifiers and stabilisers are added to some low-fat products like spreads, sauces and salad dressings to restore their original creamy texture.

Thickening agents are used to bulk out food and to make it look more solid. They, too, are usually natural substances. They include agar and carrageenan, produced from seaweed; locust bean gum, extracted from pods of the locust or carob tree; guar gum, extracted from pea seeds; and tragacanth and gum arabic, extracted from trees found in the Middle East. Further examples are xanthum gum, a by-product of corn syrup fermentation; karaya gum, extracted from trees found in South East Asia; and pectin, extracted from the leftovers of oranges and apples used in the production of orange juice and cider. They are found in a wide variety of processed foods including some low-fat options where they are used for thickening and adding the bulk originally provided by the fat. Some low-fat foods have simpless added. This is protein from milk that has been microparticulated. This fascinating-sounding process creates millions of minute balls of protein which feel to the tongue like fat. Trouble is, when heated, they solidify, like egg white, so are only suitable for use in chilled foods, like ice cream, yogurts, and salad dressing. Not all low-fat foods have anything added to replace the fat – skimmed milk and low-fat crisps for instance just have less fat.

Flavourings

You've seen the colourings, now taste the flavourings. As well as the texture, it is, after all, the taste and flavour of food that gives it its special appeal; without its natural flavour our food just wouldn't be the same. Just imagine the glorious aroma of freshly baked bread emanating from the bakery behind the bread counter and the smells emanating from an oriental restaurant, guaranteed to get the digestive juices moving. The familiar smell of burnt toast, on the other hand, stimulates not only the taste buds but also the ear with its accompaniment of a wailing smoke detector.

Most flavours are volatile and unstable and easily lost when food is cooked and stored. Reheated food rarely tastes as good as it did when first prepared. In large-scale manufacture, such as that needed to get soup into cans, treated to kill bugs, and onto a supermarket shelf, much of the original flavour of the ingredients is lost. The only answer is for the manufacturer to add the flavour – or something vaguely resembling it – back again.

There are around 2,000 different flavourings commonly added to food in the UK. The good news is that about 9 out of 10 of these are naturally occurring substances extracted from plants. Most of the remainder are identical to natural flavours, but are made artificially in the laboratory simply because it is cheaper and easier than extracting them from their natural source.

Unlike food colourings, which tend to be a single substance like beta-carotene or Sunset Yellow, most things described as a flavour on a packet or bottle of processed food are a cocktail of different chemicals. Cherry flavour, for instance, typically consists of about a dozen different flavourings mixed together in the correct proportions to produce something that tastes vaguely like cherries. It's a skilful business blending all these flavourings together to get the taste and smell you want, like creating a new perfume or blend of whisky.

Flavourings do not have E numbers and there is not the same amount of control exerted over them as there is with colourings. New flavourings are not subjected to the same rigorous testing as a new colouring or a new medicine would be. This is not quite so alarming as it might sound. Our taste buds are extremely sensitive organs and the amount of a flavouring which needs to be added to food is incredibly small, so small in most cases that it is difficult to see how they could be harmful. The average person consumes only about a teaspoonful of artificially manufactured flavourings a year. This is not to say that we should be complacent, as there may be flavourings lurking out there somewhere which are harmful in minute amounts.

Take on board the main message of this book and concentrate on eating the best of fresh foods that the supermarket has to offer and less of the processed and you will reduce your consumption of colourings and flavourings without really trying.

High Salt: Higher Blood Pressure

The additive of paramount concern to the British population is salt, as overindulgence is thought to be a major factor contributing to raised blood pressure. Most of us consume more salt than is good for us with the result that the average blood pressure of the British population is higher than it need be. The salt that we add at table or during cooking is only part of the problem. Although two out of three people still add salt to their cooking this contributes only a small part to the total salt in our diet.

Ordinary table salt, as you learned in your chemistry lessons at school, is sodium chloride. Most foods also contain another kind of salt, potassium chloride, which does not have the same effect on blood pressure as the sodium salt.

Virtually all natural food, including unprocessed cereal grains, fruit and vegetables and wild game contain more potassium than sodium, so for millions of years human beings have been eating more potassium than sodium. Today, however, in twenty-first century Britain, most of us consume more sodium than potassium and that is the main reason Brits tend to have higher blood pressure than citizens of similar age in parts of the world where salt consumption is lower.

Why is it then, if almost every kind of fresh food contains more potassium than sodium, that most of us manage to get it the wrong way round and take in more sodium that potassium? The reason will come as no surprise. It is the obvious one that so much of the food we eat isn't fresh at all. It's processed. Cornflakes are a typical example having 1,000 times more sodium than the fresh corn from which they are manufactured. They are not alone. It is the same story with most breakfast cereals although, despite the salt, cereals are still a good, energy-rich, low-fat food, full of B vitamins. So, unless you are under doctor's orders to cut down on salt, just keep enjoying them. Some have less salt than others. Weetabix, for instance, has only a third as much sodium in every 100 grams as Cornflakes, and Shredded Wheat has virtually none.

The same story repeats itself with most other foods. Crisps typically have 100 times more sodium than the same amount of baked potato. And canned vegetables and soups nearly all have loads of salt poured into them. So do cans of luncheon meat, as well as the processed meats on the meat counter, and don't forget salted butter and cheese. Avoiding high salt products like these is especially important for people who have high blood pressure, and the elderly.

We need to keep up the pressure on the food manufacturers to keep down our blood pressure by using no more sodium salt in their products than is absolutely necessary to prevent bugs from growing. It is not acceptable to add loads of salt just for the taste. To make matters even worse, during the processing most of the potassium gets leached out.

Look Before You Buy

That is the way to shop. Look before you buy! Read that label! Why spend your hard-earned cash on a salt-filled unhealthy product when an identical healthier option is sitting on the shelf right next to it? You find this all the time – virtually identical products side by side on the shelf, but one with more salt or more fat or more sugar added to it. Remember the baked beans saga. Always go for the healthy option. It takes a little more time initially to read the labels and compare brands, but once you have worked out which is the healthier option you can head straight for it next time.

Don't Tar All Additives with the Same Brush

Despite their bad press, it becomes clear that not all additives are bad for us. They are not all artificial, way-out things like the coal tar dyes in sweeties. Some additives are even positively beneficial in themselves, like E300, Vitamin C.

Ideally, all of the food we eat should be fresh and there should be no need for preservatives, but this is very difficult to achieve in today's densely populated, hungry world. In general, the health risk associated with food infested with moulds and bacteria is likely to be greater than that associated with the careful use of preservatives. On the other hand the safety of certain preservatives, like nitrites, does cause concern, and we are always wise to choose the fresh option when there is one available.

Salt and sugar are the most traditional additives used in the preservation of food. Jam, for instance, would soon go mouldy if it were not for the high concentration of sugar it contains. But excessive amounts of salt and sugar, as you know, are not healthy, and much of the sugar and salt in our food today is there purely to stimulate the taste buds, not to kill micro-organisms. Too much salt can result in high blood pressure and too much sugar in tooth decay and obesity.

When there is a good reason for additives and they have been proven to be safe they may well be acceptable. What offends, however, is the use of additives purely for cosmetic reasons, to create pretty colours in sweets, or to impart horrid flavours to fizzy drinks. Almost all of the added colourings and flavourings have absolutely no nutritional value. Although some are completely natural substances, others are completely unnatural and may even be harmful to people who are susceptible to them. It makes sense, therefore, to avoid as far as possible products that have too many unnecessary additives. Generally, the more heavily processed a food is, the more additives it is likely to contain.

Chapter 18

How to Avoid Food Poisoning

Serious outbreaks of food poisoning resulting from mass-produced foods are surprisingly rare when you consider the incredible number of products on sale and their diverse origins. It is all down to the very careful adherence to rules governing the preparation and storage of products by manufacturers, suppliers, and supermarkets alike. OK, that's a bit too rosy a picture but, despite the odd cowboys, they don't do so badly really. It would be a pity if, after all of this trouble has been taken by everyone on our behalf, that once the food was in our possession we dropped our guard and allowed it to become contaminated with bacteria and then let them grow unchecked and end up poisoning us.

The Bugs that Cause Food Poisoning

The most common type of food poisoning is caused by bacteria being inadvertently allowed to grow on food, usually meat and meat products. Some kinds of bacteria, of which the best known is the common Salmonella, and the rarer E coli 0157 can, if consumed along with our food, take up temporary residence in our intestines, increase vastly in numbers and produce an unpleasant infection. Other types of bacteria, like Staphylococcus, have a different strategy. As they grow on meat they produce toxins, and it is these toxins rather than the bacteria themselves, which make us ill.

Secret Agent 0157

A few words about this new menace Secret Agent 0157. Scientists in the United States first recognised Secret Agent 0157 as a cause of human disease in 1982. It is one of hundreds of strains of E coli, the vast majority of which are harmless. E coli is present naturally in all our intestines, where along with other micro-organisms it helps us to digest our food and even to produce certain vitamins. Where strain 0157 originally came from no one knows for certain. But instead of being a good neighbour and enjoying a give and take relationship with us like normal E coli, Secret Agent 0157 starts vandalizing the inside of our guts, and gives us violent diarrhoea. It can even threaten our lives by going on to damage our blood system and kidneys. What causes us greatest concern is that young children are most susceptible to the severest form of the disease, and that a high proportion of those who die from the condition are children.

You may wonder what the 'E.' in E coli stands for – epidemic, evil? No, disappointingly, it is 'Escherichia', after a scientist by the name of Escherich who in 1885 first isolated and characterised the bacterium. Not surprisingly, therefore, people of average articulatory agility prefer to refer to it simply as E coli.

Preventing Food from Becoming Contaminated in the First Place

The most important thing to remember is that there is a significant possibility that raw meat, poultry and eggs will be contaminated with bacteria when you buy them. The reason that meat-eaters are not constantly going down with food poisoning is that cooking meat kills bacteria dead. If, however, before cooking raw meat you allow its resident population of bacteria to contaminate meat or other dishes that have already been cooked, you are heading for trouble. If you then leave the newly contaminated meal at room temperature, the bacteria may well grow on it and poison you when you innocently consume them and their toxins along with the meal. You get the drift. Raw meat contains bacteria, and they must be prevented from escaping from it to contaminate other food. On purchasing meat and poultry, wrap it separately to prevent it from contaminating anything else, and keep it separate until the bacteria are killed by cooking.

Your Kitchen – The Main Battle Ground

The following briefing applies equally to the commercial kitchen in a factory or restaurant serving hundreds of meals a day as to the kitchen in your own home. Everyone who handles food, whether as a chef, retailer, or busy househusband, should be trained in the principles of food hygiene. So said Professor Hugh Pennington in the report he prepared for the UK government following Britain's biggest outbreak of E coli 0157 in Lanarkshire in 1996. He recommended that this training should begin in school. So if you want to be up to helping your kids with their homework join the Anti-Bug Squad now. The Fat-Tooths and their kids are welcome recruits.

So chaps, if we are to succeed in our fight against Salmonella, Secret Agent 0157 and other food poisoning organisms wherever they may be lurking – in the restaurant or in the home – we must start with the assumption that all raw meat has the enemy concealed on its surface. It probably does. While the odds are against the enemy being Secret Agent 0157, the meat may well be contaminated with other more common causes of food poisoning like Salmonella and Campylobacter.

Keep in mind the possibility of surface contamination by food-poisoning bacteria and, with a little thought, the precautions you need to take to prevent them infiltrating other foods soon become self evident.

Hitching a Lift on Utensils and Work Surfaces

Place raw meat on a plate and bacteria present on the surface of the meat are likely to stick to the plate. Then put cooked meat or even vegetables onto the contaminated plate and they are likely to become contaminated too. Similarly, if you cut raw meat with a knife and then use the same knife to cut cooked meat, bacteria may well be transported on the knife from the raw to the cooked meat, on which, if they are kept warm, they may proceed to grow. Wash utensils and work areas that have come into contact with raw meat thoroughly with hot soapy water and disinfectant before using them to prepare other food items. Preferably, have two sets of utensils, one for preparing raw meat and another for other types of food. In restaurant kitchens it is essential to have one work surface for handling raw meat and another work surface for cooked and other foods, and to use colour coded utensils to make sure that the two sets of utensils are always kept separate.

Keep Those Hands Clean

Don't forget your hands. They are constantly becoming contaminated with bacteria from a variety of sources and great care has to be taken to ensure that harmful bacteria do not hitch a lift on them to food. Hands should always be washed before preparing food and in particular, after:

- handling raw meat
- going to the lavatory
- emptying waste bins
- handling pets
- blowing your nose
- touching your face or hair

When preparing food, always wash your hands after handling unwashed raw vegetables and, in particular, **after handling raw meat**. Pets, especially dogs, always have their noses into something, and the more enthusiastic amongst them even gain immense pleasure from rolling in it. The last two precautions on the list are not so much directed at Salmonella and Secret Agent 0157 as at Staphylococcus aureus, which is carried on the skin and up the noses of over a third of adults.

Wash hands thoroughly with hot soapy water, paying particular attention to nails, areas around rings and between fingers. Then dry your hands on a **clean** towel. It is best not to wear rings when preparing food as bacteria tend to accumulate on the skin underneath them.

Dish Towels that are Dirty

Beware of oven gloves, dish towels and cloths that you use to lift food and to dry dishes as they tend to be a hotbed of bacterial activity. The safest way of drying dishes is to allow the water to drain and then evaporate off; it is also the easiest, and thus the method favoured by Mr Fat-Tooth and Mr Trim-Guy alike. In catering establishments, the use of towels for drying dishes and utensils is generally discouraged. If you do use them in the home, be sure to replace with a clean one at least every day, and don't use the same towel for drying dishes that you used for putting raw meat into the oven.

Always use a separate towel for drying your hands on after washing them. Do not contaminate your nice clean hands with bacteria by drying them on the dishtowel you have just used for handling raw meat. Similarly, after handling raw meat, don't wipe your hands on a towel that might later be used for drying dishes. Wash your hands in hot soapy water first. Needless to say, wiping bloodstained hands on an apron is not to be recommended. Wash them first in hot soapy water.

The Unique Hazards of the Domestic Kitchen

Kitchens in catering establishments are used for preparing food, and for that purpose alone. In contrast, in the home, due to lack of space, they frequently double as a washroom, or even as a kennel for the dog and cat. If your washing machine is in the kitchen you will be bringing contaminated clothing, including underwear contaminated with traces of faeces, into an area which should be scrupulously clean. It is so very easy to inadvertently put this clothing onto a work surface, forgetting that it will later be used for preparing food. Make sure you don't make this mistake, especially if you take in other people's washing, and always wash your hands after loading the washing machine and before preparing food.

It is not acceptable to keep pets in the kitchen as they have a habit of climbing and getting their noses everywhere. There must be somewhere else that they can go.

Hands that do Dishes

Little girl: "Mummy, why are your hands so soft?"

Her father, interrupting: "Because your Daddy does all the washing up."

We do the washing up every day so we might as well learn how to do it properly. If you don't have an automatic dishwasher, or if you are the automatic dishwasher, here is an effective method using a double-sink.

✔ Scrape off surplus food into the bin. This should be foot-operated so that you don't contaminate your fingers on opening it.

✔ Wash the items in detergent and hot water in the main sink. The detergent removes food particles and bacteria from the plate and the heat helps to kill them. Use rubber gloves to protect your hands from the heat.

✔ Use a nylon brush with a plastic handle to clean the plates. These are better than cloths and foam pads that tend to pick up particles of food and become breeding grounds for bacteria.

✔ Fill the second sink with very hot water. Rinse the items in it and leave them there for about two minutes. The hot water will kill most of the remaining bacteria and heat the items so that they dry more quickly.

✔ Remove the items from the rinse sink and leave them to dry in air on a clean draining tray. If your wife insists that you dry them with a cloth, tell her I said it was unhygienic. How about that for solidarity?

As if washing dishes isn't a chore enough, remember that our kitchens, especially the work surfaces, need to be kept scrupulously clean. An ordinary household disinfectant like common bleach, diluted in hot water as recommended by the manufacturer, does the job as chlorine is released from it killing the bacteria. Disinfectants work best in hot water and the heat itself helps to kill bacteria. Like dishes, it is preferable if work surfaces are left to dry naturally by evaporation rather than running the risk of contaminating them with dirty drying cloths.

I am very much in favour of separate water heaters for the sink and the bath so that small volumes of very hot water are available exclusively for washing up, with the thermostat in the bath water heater set at a lower temperature. This is more energy efficient that having one big tank of hot water for both, and eliminates the danger of boiling bath water, especially if the household includes young children and the elderly.

Fridges and freezers also have to be cleaned regularly. Most people use bicarbonate of soda rather than bleach, which tends to taint food. Take care when cleaning the fridge that the temperature of the food you remove in the process does not rise too high for too long so that it becomes a breeding ground for bacteria.

Anal Effluent as a Source of Food Poisoning

Faeces, both human and animal, are a potent source of Salmonella that may be transferred to food via unwashed hands, dogs' noses or flies' feet. Eggs may be contaminated directly by the birds that laid them. Tortoises and turtles are usually infected with nasty strains of Salmonella, so if you have any of these pets around, be sure to wash your hands thoroughly after handling them.

The biggest menaces of all, though, are human carriers of nasty strains of Salmonella and other harmful gut bacteria who fail to wash their hands after going to the lavatory and thereby manage to initiate large-scale outbreaks of food poisoning amongst the customers of the canteens, restaurants and shops where they work.

How to Survive a Trip to the Toilet

Most toilet blocks are so badly designed, it's unbelievable. To start with, there are always too few ladies' toilets. More importantly, from the healthy eating viewpoint, the layout seems designed to maximise the risk of food poisoning rather than to prevent it. You discharge the day's waste, then on turning on the tap to wash your hands, you contaminate it with bacteria from your intestines. After washing your hands in disinfected soap you then have to turn the contaminated tap off, during which process your own intestinal bacteria and those of other toilet users are transferred from the tap back onto your nice clean hands.

Some public toilets have taps that you push down to initiate the flow of water and that subsequently turn themselves off automatically. Unfortunately, this usually happens before you have time to get your hands underneath. As a result, you end up holding the contaminated tap down with one hand whilst attempting to wash your other hand in the trickle of water emanating from it.

To prevent this fiasco, taps should be operated by a foot pump beneath the wash basin that you press to eject water, or a photoelectric sensor that turns the tap on as your hands approach and off again as they depart. Such taps are rare. So, many decades after setting foot on the moon, it should not be beyond the wit of man to devise a reliable, pollution-free method of turning off toilet taps, and opening doors.

Dirty Door Handles

The outside door leading to the ladies or gents is the next hurdle. Why do they always have handles? These are contaminated both by hands that were not washed after using the toilet as well as by hands that were washed and then became contaminated again on turning off the tap. Health conscious toilet goers should be able to open the outer door to escape from the toilet just by pushing it, without having to turn a dirty handle. Scraps of paper can be used to turn off taps and open doors, but the problem is where to get them from and what to do with them after, especially if hot air dryers are provided instead of paper towels and waste bins.

Many people on entering a restaurant go to the toilet before eating, thereby ensuring that they have enough bacteria on their hands to contaminate any food they happen to touch before putting it into their mouths. The number of bacterial cells picked up from taps and handles may not in itself be enough to produce most kinds of food poisoning and, as the food will be eaten immediately, they will not have the chance to multiply on it. An exception is Secret Agent 0157, the E coli superbug, the infectious dose of which is so low – some experts say as few as ten cells – that infection by this route is a real possibility.

A serious problem can arise if catering staff using equally badly designed toilets transfer salmonella and other bacteria from their contaminated hands onto cooked meat. If the bacteria have the time and warmth to multiply before the food is served, the result can be a coach load of very unhappy holidaymakers, especially if the coach has only one toilet. The same risk applies to food shops of course. The architects who design toilet blocks should go back to first principles – Lego bricks!

Cool It!

The second line of defence is to keep meat products at a low temperature and consume them as soon as possible, before bacteria have a chance to grow. That will appeal to Mr Fat-Tooth, "I'll just finish off those hamburgers, dear, before the bacteria multiply and give us food poisoning." Deep freezing is the answer to such treachery. In deep frozen meat, bacteria, although not necessarily killed, cannot increase in numbers. Even at a normal fridge temperature of between 0 and 5 degrees Celsius they multiply very slowly, if at all.

Check Out that Fridge

But are you sure that the temperature of your fridge is low enough, really certain. If not, buy a fridge thermometer and find out. Discover what that silly dial numbered 1 to 6 means in actual degrees Centigrade (or Celsius if you want to honour its inventor). It's incredible that most fridges come without an built-in thermometer; it's like supplying a car without a speedometer. The international standard for the internal temperature of refrigerators is 5 degrees Celsius. As warm air rises, the top of the fridge tends to be a bit warmer than this and the bottom a bit cooler. Place the thermometer on the

top shelf, the warmest part, for about two hours. If the temperature is more than 5 or 6 degrees Celsius, adjust the dial to get a lower temperature. Remember the temperature only has to rise a few degrees above 5 for most kinds of bacteria to start multiplying, so check it out today. Now to nip out and buy shares in a company which manufactures fridge thermometers in anticipation of this book becoming a best-seller.

At room temperature bacteria multiply much faster than they do in a fridge, and next to a central heating radiator, or in the boot of a car on a warm day, they can really get going. When doing the week's shopping in the supermarket, chilled and frozen foods should be selected last so that they have less time to thaw out before we get them home and safely into the fridge. If you are not intending to head off home immediately, it is a good idea, if they are to be left in the warm boot of a car for any length of time, to use a cool bag or box with ice cubes.

Don't put hot food into a fridge. Food cooked for eating later should be cooled as quickly as possible in a cold place, and once it is cool, then placed in the fridge. Placing it in the fridge straight away might increase the temperature of the fridge, and in the time it takes for it to get back down to its proper temperature bacteria may have started to grow on the food that is already there.

Avoiding Cross Contamination

Refrigeration unfortunately brings its own dangers. With different kinds of food packed so closely together in the refrigerator, cross contamination from raw meat to other foods can easily take place. Catering establishments should have a separate refrigerator for raw meat. If this is impracticable in the home – although a large family might consider having two small refrigerators rather than one big one – raw meat should always be kept wrapped and at the bottom of the fridge to avoid the danger of contaminated juices dripping from the raw meat onto ready-to-eat food beneath.

The Good News: Cooking Kills Bacteria, Dead

Cook raw meat thoroughly to ensure that any bacteria contaminating it are killed. Bacteria on the surface are readily disposed of by the heat of the oven, which is why direct infection from consuming joints of beef is rarer than might be expected. The problem arises when bacteria have been allowed to penetrate deep below the surface, which can easily happen when beef is ground up to make hamburgers. It is now recommended that all parts of the ground beef should reach at least 70°C when cooked, so that it is not pink at the centre and juices run clear. Also take especial care with large pieces of frozen meat. If it isn't thawed all of the way through, the centre may not be cooked enough. In poultry the bacteria are naturally at the centre, in the intestines, so cook them thoroughly.

When you want to thaw out joints of meat, the best way to do it is either in the 5-degree part of the refrigerator or, if pressed for time, in a microwave. Leaving frozen meat to thaw out for too long in a warm room may allow its temperature to rise above 5 degrees Celsius, to a point where the bacteria can start increasing in numbers.

Don't Overdo the Cooking!

In ensuring that you cook meat and poultry thoroughly to kill food poisoning bacteria, make sure that you do not overdo the roasting or grilling. Burning food generates a cocktail of obnoxious chemicals, some of which may be as potentially harmful as those in cigarette smoke. It is a wise precaution therefore to avoid eating anything that is obviously burnt, whether meat or toast. If you come across any burnt offerings, complain to the cook. If you are afraid that this might lead to you becoming a victim of domestic violence, cut them off and display them in a prominent position so that the cook gets a gentle hint!

The Bad News: Cooking Kills Bacteria but not their Toxins

The bad news is that certain kinds of bacteria produce heat resistant spores and toxins that may not be completely destroyed by cooking. The most serious kind of food poisoning is botulism caused by the bacterium Clostridium botulinum. Clostridium is what is known as an anaerobic bacterium. What this means is that it can grow in the absence of air, for example in a sealed can. Boiling up the contents of the can after we open it may kill the bacterium but not the deadly toxin it produces. It is because of Clostridium botulinum that manufacturers have to heat canned foods to such a high temperature that they lose their colour and much of their texture. Unlike most bacteria, salmonella, for example, which are easily killed by moderate temperatures such as those used in pasteurising milk, Clostridium produces spores that can only be destroyed by exposure to very high temperatures. The heat resistant spores combined with the heat resistant toxins make Clostridium the food technologist's worst enemy. There is comparatively little we can do to protect ourselves against botulism. Our life is in the hands of the manufacturers.

Staphylococcus, the bug found up people's noses and in their boils and pimples, also produces toxins on food – I hope you are not eating your lunch as you read this. Once it has had a chance to colonise a slab of meat and pump out toxins, cooking it will not prevent your guests from going down with food poisoning. Even though the bacteria itself is killed, its toxins will show no mercy.

Protecting Those Most at Risk

The Fat-Tooths and their cousins, the Trim-Guys, are strong enough to withstand a brief bout of food poisoning, so long as it is not botulism. When preparing food for young children, pregnant women, the very elderly, or anyone with low resistance to infection, however, we should be extra careful. That's why cooks in residential homes for the elderly should always be specially trained in food hygiene. Eggs should be cooked thoroughly until both the yolk and whites are solid, and any ready-cooked, chilled meals or ready-to-eat poultry that we buy should **not** be regarded as ready to eat until they have been re-cooked to zap any contaminating bacteria. For most of us, most of the time, such extreme precautions are not necessary.

To reduce the risk of Listeria, which can harm the unborn baby, women while they are pregnant should avoid eating soft, ripened cheeses of the brie, camembert or blue-vein types.

Chapter 19

A Pyramid for the Living

Please Don't Climb it Just Because it's There

Feeling fit, then it's time to set about constructing a healthy eating pyramid. I'll just go and get the whip out. The purpose of the original pyramids was to house the dead, but our 21st-century pyramid is designed to promote a long and healthy life. Start by drawing a big triangle to represent a pyramid and draw four horizontal lines through it to separate it into five levels. This assumes that your artistic ability, like mine, never progressed beyond that of a three-year-old chimpanzee with learning difficulties; otherwise you might be able to draw something a bit more convincing. While on the subject of apes, if man and woman evolved from apes, why are there still apes? Anyway, back to the pyramid.

The Starchy Base of the Pyramid

The first task is to construct a firm foundation for our pyramid. This will be formed of those energy-rich foods we need every day to provide us with the energy to keep us going. No, not fat or bags of sugar. The source of most of our energy should be starch. Bread, especially wholemeal bread, potatoes and root vegetables, breakfast cereals, rice and pasta all fit the bill. Shovel them onto the base of the pyramid. Sketch them or cut and paste pictures out of a glossy magazine, or if you are a person of the twenty-first century, cheat and use a graphics package and clip art.

As well as supplying us with energy, these starchy foods are also rich in most of the B vitamins, minerals and fibre, and contain a respectable helping of protein.

The Healthy Second Level

For the second level we need to select foods that we can also eat regularly to provide us with extra protein and vitamins to complement those in the starchy foods. For first-class protein there is poultry, fish and wild game such as venison. Vegetarians can obtain equally good protein from semi-skimmed or skimmed milk, cottage cheese, low-fat yoghurt and egg whites. And don't forget peas and beans, those essential components of the magic mixture which, combined with cereals, add up to first-class protein.

For extra vitamins and minerals, fresh fruit like apples, pears and bananas and pure fruit juices are a must, along with green vegetables. Don't forget that the greens can be either fresh or frozen.

The Once-in-a-While Third Level

This level is home to the low-fat or low sugar options of the products in the Treacherous Fourth Level, such as low-fat biscuits and low-fat crisps, oven ready chips, low-fat ice-cream or reduced-sugar jam. Small amounts of the leaner cuts of red meat with the visible fat removed, food fried in fresh vegetable oils and nuts may be placed here. Some healthy option ready-made meals will also find a home here.

The Treacherous Fourth Level

The fourth level of your pyramid is for the traditional high fat, high sugar brands of cakes, biscuits, sticky puddings, chocolates, crisps, chips, jam and marmalade, sweets and ice cream. This level will also harbour most pig, cow and sheep products – the Fearsome Fat Three. No, the occasional "lean" joint of red meat won't do you any harm but, so as not to overdose on sat fats, steer clear of processed meats like sausages, meat pies, mince, burgers and luncheon meats most of the time. Once or twice a week is quite enough. Don't forget to put cans of beer here too. Alcohol is very fattening. Most ready-made meals fit into this category.

The Pyramid's Slippery Peak

Now for the slippery slope leading to the top of the pyramid which only kamikaze eaters should attempt to scale. The peak is the home of products that we should eat as little of as possible, mainly because they contain too much slimy, slippery, saturated fat, the downfall of so many intrepid consumers.

At the peak of the pyramid are also to be found full-fat dairy products such as butter, cream, full-fat milk and full-fat cheese. Avoid them and partake of the semi-skimmed and skimmed milk and low-fat cheeses on the second and third levels instead.

Food fried in lard and butter is also up there. This method of frying should be completely abandoned in favour of vegetable oil, non-stick pans, boiling, grilling or microwaving.

Salt is up there too. It pervades processed food, so don't add even more in cooking or at the table, unless you plan to be digging holes in the road in the heat of the midday sun or sweating profusely for some other reason.

Healthy Eating means Increased Variety, not Less

Now stand back and survey your pyramid, casting yours eyes up towards the peak and you will see just how few forbidden foods there are. It is a common misconception that healthy eating means depriving ourselves. On the contrary, it simply means eating more of the healthy, fresh foods at the bottom of the pyramid and not so much of the high fat, high sugar and high salt products higher up. More excitingly, it means keeping our eyes and ears open for new healthy items and recipes to enrich our eating.

Fully steeped in the principles of a healthy diet, as you encounter other foods you will now know where they fit on the pyramid, whether you should incorporate them into your weekly diet, just partake once in a while or shun them completely.

But I Can't Afford to Buy Healthy Food

The Fat-Tooths claim that they don't eat healthy food because it's too expensive. How do they make that out? You and I know that bread is healthier than cake and biscuits. It is much cheaper too. Poultry is healthier than red meat and costs about half as much. Raw potatoes are healthier than chips and crisps yet only a fraction of the price. For a quick snack, a fresh Golden Delicious is healthier than a fried Golden Wonder and

A PYRAMID FOR THE LIVING

about half the price. Bread without butter is healthier than bread with butter, and obviously cheaper. Tap water is as nutritious as fizzy drinks full of flavours and additives and it costs virtually nothing. Potatoes, swedes, carrots, brown rice and pasta are all inexpensive sources of vitamins and energy-yielding carbohydrate. I could go on and on.

No, Mr and Mrs Fat-Tooth, that old excuse just will not do. Fruit and vegetables may appear expensive, but remember that they contain the sort of nutrients, vitamins, minerals and fibre that you need more of. In contrast, the cakes, biscuits, chips and chocolate bars that you are filling up on instead largely consist of nutrients that you would benefit from consuming less of, like saturated fat, sugar and salt.

I hope I have succeeded in convincing you that fresh food is a good buy. But what about the cost of healthy varieties of the same food; skimmed milk compared with full-fat milk, or baked beans without added sugar compared with baked beans with added sugar? Compare the prices of healthy, low sugar, low-fat varieties of processed foods in your local grocery store with the less healthy, high sugar, high fat versions and see if there is any difference. I bet you will find that the healthy option is usually no more expensive than the unhealthy. One notable exception is bread, the cheapest wholemeal usually costing about a third more than the cheapest white. On the other hand, standard breakfast cereals like cornflakes sell for about a third less than their sugary equivalents.

The Virtues of a Varied Diet

Remember, aspiring Mr and Mrs Trim-Guy, that there is nothing better than a well-balanced varied diet. And by 'well balanced', I don't mean a hamburger in each hand. Healthy eating, far from being boring, opens up new opportunities, encouraging us to enrich our eating with foods we haven't tried before. The French, remember, have one of the world's healthiest diets, and who would dare to describe French cuisine as boring!

Most importantly, avoid at all cost those kamikaze diets which so many of our fellow citizens adhere to, like Mr Fat-Tooth's Meat Pie, Chips and Lager Diet, or Mrs Fat-Tooth's, Cake With Everything Diet, or the Fat-Tooth Kid's Crisps, Fizzy Drinks and Snack Bar Diet.

At the other extreme, don't you or your partner go overboard on so-called 'health foods'. Don't consume unnaturally large amounts of the latest miracle ingredient, to the exclusion of other food, just because you are persuaded by the hype into thinking it holds the key to eternal youth or the dissolving of cellulite. That is exactly what people did in the past with milk and butter and that is a mistake we definitely don't want to make again.

No sweat, Mr and Mrs Fat-Tooth. Eat plenty of fresh fruit, green vegetables, fish and poultry, drink semi-skimmed milk, and get most of your energy from starchy foods like root vegetables and cereals instead of from fatty foods like red meat, cake and biscuits and, when you next shed your outer layers, the beautiful Mr and Mrs Trim-Guy will emerge.

And Plenty of Regular Exercise

If you are really serious about losing weight, want to cast off the Fat-Tooth image and become the new Trim-Guys, combine healthy eating with more exercise. Go for the complete package, not just a healthy diet but a healthy lifestyle. Scientists have shown that, just as with healthy eating, regular exercise reduces the risk of coronary heart disease, high blood pressure and osteoporosis, and by burning off the excess calories, helps us to avoid becoming overweight and obese. Lack of exercise is not just a problem for the Brits; it is estimated that half of the world's population now take too little exercise. Labour saving devices in the home and in the workplace have greatly reduced the amount of regular daily exercise, and now that most people drive to work instead of walking, even to the bus stop, millions get virtually no exercise from one week to the next.

Towards the close of the last millennium, the World Health Organisation and the International Federation of Sports Medicine got together to issue recommendations regarding the minimum amount of exercise we should be taking. This is what they came up with.

✔ 'Daily physical activity should be accepted as the cornerstone of a healthy lifestyle. Physical activity should be reintegrated into the routine of everyday living. An obvious first step would be the use of stairs instead of lifts, and walking or cycling for short journeys.'

✔ 'Adults should be encouraged to increase habitual physical activity gradually, aiming to carry out every day at least 30 minutes of physical activity of moderate intensity e.g. brisk walking and stair climbing. More strenuous activities such as slow jogging, cycling, field and court games (soccer, tennis etc.) and swimming could provide additional benefits.'

✔ 'The fact that there are benefits to be gained by starting physical activity at any age should be *broadcast* more widely.'

OK, so here is the 11 o'clock news. "Get off your backside and get some exercise. So say the world's leading fitness experts."

Note carefully the words **at least** 30 minutes of physical activity each day. If you walk to work or jog occasionally, you will probably be taking this amount of exercise anyway. In that case, why not set your sights higher still to become even fitter, and do not just one, but two, thirty-minute stints a day.

At the opposite end of the spectrum, if you are very sedentary start with gentle walking and build up gradually over a period of months. You don't have to rush but you must be persistent. Remember your car is not like a dog needing its daily walkies; it doesn't need to be taken for a drive every day. But you, like the dog, do need a daily walkies. Build up the distance and speed gradually and you will be surprised what you can achieve over a comparatively short period. Perhaps to start with you will only be going at 100 steps per minute, then over the weeks you will get up to 110, then 120, 130, 140 and maybe even break the 150 barrier. Once you get into top gear there will be no stopping you. Remember, you can walk as fast as you like without any fear of losing your licence.

Plenty of brisk walking, jogging, golf or other ball games, swimming, dancing, exercise classes, workouts to videos, weight training – whatever you and your partner enjoy doing – will help you to get the most out of all this good food. Go for it man!

Chapter 20

A Happy Ending

Every book should have a happy ending, and if you are the sort of person who is always finding it a bit of a struggle to avoid putting on weight, here is one for you!

Eat More Without Putting on Weight!

Pork pie in the sky surely! Not at all. It is made possible by two key facts. Fact number one: a gram of fat yields twice as many calories as a gram of starch (fat has 9 kcal in a gram compared with starch's 4 kcal). Fact number two: starchy foods like potatoes are more bulky than fatty foods like butter. The combined result is that a pound of potatoes provides only one tenth as many calories as a pound of butter. So by cutting down on fatty foods and increasing your intake of fresh fruit and vegetables you can actually eat more without putting on weight!

The Kilocalorie Counter

Energy in the United Kingdom is measured in kilocalories. To save suffering repetitive strain injury writing out 'kilocalories' all the time it is usually abbreviated to 'kcal', which is what you see on food labels. In other European countries energy is measured in Joules, which also appears on food labels here, but it is too confusing to use both measures. So with all due respect to citizen Joules, we are best to stick with kcal. Kilocalories is a bit of a mouthful and 'kcal' awkward to get the tongue around, so people usually talk about calories, but as commonly used they mean the same thing.

Look at the table alongside. It shows that fat, that most calorie-dense of foods, yields over twice as many kcal as the same weight of carbohydrate or protein. Although we tend to think of protein as a muscle builder, if we consume more than we need, the excess can be used to provide

Sources of Energy

Source	kcal in each 100g (3.5 ounces)
Fat	900
Carbohydrate (i.e. Starch and Sugar)	400
Protein	400
Alcohol	700

energy. Unless we are teetotal, from time to time – hopefully not from opening to closing – we will obtain calories from alcohol. Note that 100ml of pure alcohol have almost as many calories as 100g of pure fat, so, is alcohol fattening? I'll say it is!

How much energy we need each day depends on our age. It also depends on sex. (I mean whether we are male or female, although the other interpretation affects energy demand as well.) It depends, too, on our size, how active we are, as well as on our individual metabolism. A manual or womanual (no effort is spared to ensure political correctness) worker or sportsman or sportswoman for instance will require more energy, all else being equal, than an office worker who drives their VW to their PC, then back home again to their TV.

The next table warns us how many calories to expect from consuming 100g of each of the main types of food. The contrast between the high calorie foods in the left hand column and the low calorie in the right is striking.

CALORIES AT A GLANCE

The Fat-Tooth's Favourites	Kcal in each 100g of food	The making of the Trim-Guys	Kcal in each 100g of food
Beer	800 (in 6 cans)	Breakfast cereals	350
Butter	800	Bread	200
Margarine	700	Fatty fish	200
Nuts	600	Chicken and turkey	150
Crisps	550	White fish	100
Biscuits	500	Typical low-fat yoghurts	100
Snack bars	500	Root vegetables	50
Cheese	400	Fruit	30
Most red meats	250-400	Green vegetables	25
Cakes	350		

The next table gives an indication of the amounts of energy required by children and adults based on figures from the Ministry of Agriculture, Fisheries and Food.

Consume more food than you can use and what happens to it? Excess fat is stored as fat; that's pretty obvious, but what about excess carbohydrate and protein? We can store small amounts of extra carbohydrate in our liver as a kind of carbohydrate known as glycogen, but we convert the rest into fat. The same goes for excess protein, which we also convert into fat and store for a rainy day.

As you can see from the table, women tend to use their food more efficiently than men, extracting more useful energy from the ounce, and so need to consume less. This applies even if they are of the same weight and indulge in a similar level of activity. You may wonder why I've included a figure for men during pregnancy. Well men have a lot of extra running around to do when their wives are pregnant, don't they? This figure is just a fun guestimate, not a serious calculation by the Men from the Ministry.

Maintaining a constant weight means balancing intake against activity. To reduce weight we need to consume less kcal than our daily need so that we start to draw upon our fat stores to make up the deficit. But in keeping down our kcal intake don't fall for the Seven Deadly Misconceptions of Mr Fat-Tooth. No, I am not referring to the girls he accidentally got pregnant, but to his failure to recognise the existence of calories in certain situations. For example:

✔ If he eats something and no one sees him eat it, it has no calories.

✔ When drinking a diet fizzy drink along with a packet of crisps or chocolate bar, the calories in the crisps or chocolate bar are cancelled by the diet fizzy drink.

✔ When he eats with someone else, calories don't count as long as he doesn't eat more than they do.

Estimated Average Daily Energy Requirements in the UK. (to the nearest 100 kcal). Warning: these figures are averages. Our actual energy requirements will depend on our size and individual metabolism and how active we are.

Age and activity	Males, Kcal per day	Females, Kcal per day
Children; increases gradually with age		
1 to 3 years	1200	1200
7 to 10 years	2000	1700
11 to 14 years	2200	1800
15 to 18 years	2800	2100
Adults		
19 to 59 years	2500	1900
60 to 74 years	2300	1900
Over 75	2100	1800
Pregnancy	2800!	2100

✔ Foods used for medicinal purposes never count e.g. brandy, hot chocolate, dry toast.

✔ If he fattens up everyone else around him, he will become thinner.

✔ TV and cinema related foods do not have calories as they are part of the entertainment package and not part of one's personal diet e.g. chocolate buttons, buttered popcorn, boiled sweets, and cans of lager.

✔ If he or his partner are in the process of preparing something, food licked off knives and spoons have no calories e.g. peanut butter on a knife, ice cream on a spoon.

Food is an Essential Component of a Balanced Diet

Nowhere in the world has more food available to eat, and nowhere has more diets to prevent us from eating it. Some of these diets are way out and of no proven effectiveness, but many more, while effective if adhered to, are far too complex, going into great detail regarding what should and should not be eaten at each meal, and have zero chance of being adhered to.

You have a slim chance (or is it a fat chance) of losing weight permanently if you go on a crash diet for a few months and at the end of it return to the same pattern of eating you practised at the beginning. Faced with what it thinks is a period of starvation, your body responds as it would during a drought or other real period of food shortage by using what little food it has coming in more efficiently. Then when you stop your diet and resume eating as you did before, your body will continue to utilise its food more efficiently and store the excess as fat. By the time it realises that the period of starvation is over, you will be Mr and Mrs Fat-Tooth again.

However, if you are so fat that when you take a shower your feet stay dry, you certainly need to lose weight. If you want to lose weight, or to avoid putting it on, cut down on the fat first. Not only is too much saturated fat harmful in itself, but all kinds of fat as we have seen, contain over twice as many calories as the same weight of starch or sugar. Always go for the low-fat options.

If your car is designed to run on petrol, would you fill its tank with diesel fuel? A diet high in saturated fat is not the fuel our bodies were designed to run on. And remember, if you are trying to lose weight, the scales should not be hidden away in the bathroom. They should be by the fridge as a constant reminder!

The only way to ensure that the fat stays off is to keep the calories down to a sensible level for ever more, but this can be achieved by healthy eating, with all-out dieting a thing of the past! Remember though that a good habit is much easier to get out of than a bad one, so keep hard at it.

Eat, Drink and be Merry, for Tomorrow you Diet

No, you don't have to stop eating and drinking anything to adopt a healthy diet; just get the balance right. I know that many people's idea of a balanced diet is a hamburger in each hand, but you know better. It's not going to be so bad as you think. Once people stop leaping out of the way every time that your pager goes off, thinking that you are about to reverse, you will know that it has all been worth while.

Bye Bye, Mr and Mrs Fat-Tooth

That's about it, Mr and Mrs Fat-Tooth. Next time we meet, the hand that I shake will be that of Mr and Mrs Trim-Guy. If you have enjoyed reading this book, and had a good laugh, tell your friends they should get a copy. If not, just use your mouth for healthy eating. Be seeing you, Trim-Guys!

Index